MORE PRAISE FOR
AN UNUSED INTELLIGENCE

"Physical thinking practices are a profound way
to transform theory into reality."

*—Lorraine MacIver, Project Manager,
Corporate Development Agriculture Canada*

"Andy Bryner and Dawna Markova's use of physical thinking is an
essential tool for corporate America. They are teaching a way for
businesspeople to frame their day-to-day situation. I was curious
about corporate America's reception to physical thinking. The
response was overwhelmingly positive. One executive told me that
the physical learning activities were the most important part of
a learning seminar he recently attended."

*—Dave Meador, Manager, Financial and Performance
Measurements, Chrysler Corporation*

"If you think learning occurs only in our heads as most of us are
taught to believe, this book opens up a whole new realm of
exploration and possibility. For those of us who have had the
opportunity to experience them, the embodiment practices taught
by Dawna and Andy have provided access to the profound
yet largely untapped wisdom of the body."

*—Jeff Clanon, Executive Director,
MIT Center for Organizational Learning*

"This easily readable book gently points the way for all of us to
re-discover and apply the unused intelligence we all possess but forgot."

*—Herb Rau, Total Quality Manager,
National Semiconductor*

"Dawna and Andy's teachings have helped me to understand a learning capacity through physical actions that I never knew I had. There is no question that it has made me and those with whom I have applied it more effective!"

—April Flanagan, Vice President, Human Resources, Philips Display Components

"This book offers ideas and practices that will guide you to balance and health in your life and your organization. It is more than a book; it is a study guide that fosters deep learning through inquiry, reflection, and practice."

—Rita Cleary, President, The Learning Circle

"Too often the input for 'learning' is limited to auditory and visual stimulation. Unfortunately, this excludes a critical component of how we learn—physical learning. After all, this is how we learn to play sports or music, or drive a car. Andy Bryner and Dawna Markova offer an important antidote to this problem with AN UNUSED INTELLIGENCE."

—Herb Rau, Total Quality Manager, National Semiconductor

"Get ready to start your motor, Andy & Dawna will take you on a whole new trip with this book. Hang on! This book addresses the whole in you—physical, mental, spiritual. You will feel good all over."

—BC Huselton, Vice President Human and Business Systems, GS Technologies

AN UNUSED

INTELLIGENCE

AN UNUSED INTELLIGENCE

PHYSICAL THINKING FOR 21ST CENTURY LEADERSHIP

ANDY BRYNER & DAWNA MARKOVA, Ph.D.

Foreword by Peter Senge, author of *The Fifth Discipline*

CONARI PRESS
Berkeley, California

Conari Press books are distributed by Publishers Group West.

Cover Design: Shelley Firth
Matrix: Jane LaPointe
Photos: Michael Goodman: Practices 2, 5, 8, 14, 17–1, 20
Donald E. McIlraith: Practices 11, 17–2

ISBN: 0-943233-97-6

Library of Congress Cataloging-in-Publication Data
Bryner, Andy.
    An unused intelligence : physical thinking for 21st century leadership /
    Andy Bryner & Dawna Markova ; foreword by Peter Senge.
        p.   cm.
    Includes bibliographical references and index.
    ISBN 0–943233–97–6 (trade paper)
    1. Organizational effectiveness.   2. Leadership.   3. Work groups.
I. Markova, Dawna, 1942–   II. Title.
HD58.82.B78   1996   95–41283

Printed in the United States of America on recycled paper.

10 9 8 7 6 5 4 3 2 1

Dedication

In Hawaii, if you are fresh from the mainland, a little too bright and quick, and ask for instructions from an islander on how to catch crabs, you will be told: "Carry a bucket with you. After you have grabbed the first one, put it in your pocket. Keep it there until you grab the second crab. Then put them both in the bottom of the bucket."

Most of us from the mainland ask the inevitable question, "Why don't you put the first crab into the bucket?" The islander will flash a wide, loose smile and reply, "Because if you do, it will crawl right out. But if you put in two, when one begins to climb the walls, the second will pull it right back down to the bottom again. So if you have at least two or more in your bucket, you never have to worry about any of them getting out!"

This book is dedicated to those of us who wish to find a way to support each other's climb out of the hidden buckets of limited thinking and gaze upon the vast horizon.

In Appreciation to Those Who Supported Our Climb:

Morihei Ueshiba
Koichi Tohei
Terry Dobson
Richard Kuboyama
Shinichi Suzuki
Lloyd Miyashiro
Dean Mayer
Glenn T. Nitta
Stefan Schweitzer
Mary Heiny
Peter Davis
Hugh Young
Aaron Ward
Shogo Yodogawa
Josh Silman

Edward Bales
Sara Norton
Ken Nisson

Moshė Feldenkrais
Ruth Alon
Ilana Rubenfeld
Milton Ericskon, M.D.
Thich Nhat Hanh
Rita Cleary
Peter Senge
Jeff Clanon
Linda Booth
George Roth

David A. Peck

Anne Powell
Jane LaPointe
June LaPointe
Dale Lowery
Peris Gumz
Jerry Cimmet
Sarah Helfman
Denys Candy
Leslie Pollitt
Frances Wong
Shauna Mae Frazier
Tamara McFall

Michael Goodman
Don McIlraith
Will Glennon
Emily Miles
Ame Beanland
Jennifer Brontsema

Judy Sorum Brown
Juanita Brown

David Issacs
Riki Moss
Lonnie Weiss

And those who have called us "teacher."

In Appreciation For Contributions To This Book:

Barbara Bauer

Dave Bazetta

Rick Bowles III

Jim Bradley

Bill Brenneman

Bill O'Brien

Sheila Busz

Susan Dupre

Jane Esper

Andy Ezzell

April Flanagan

Lester Heath

Bea Mah Holland

Elizabeth Holmes

B.C. Huselton

Brian Joiner

Laurie Joiner

Charles Kiefer

Fred Kofman

Dave Marsing

Dave Meador

Dan Mlakar

Renee Moorefield

Bill Mullin

Herb Rau

Sara Schley

Eric Siegel

Kathy Speck-Rossi

Rich Teerlink

Jean Tully

Iva Wilson

Bud Wonsiewicz

Jim Young

And to the one who never believed in buckets to begin with:

Mary Jane Ryan

Contents

RELATING YOUR QUESTIONS TO THE PRACTICES

	1	2	3	4	5	6	7	8	9	10	11	12	13	14	15	16	17	18	19	20	21
THE FIVE DISCIPLINES																					
Mental Models			⟳	⟳	⟳	⟳				⟳	⟳		⟳						⟳	⟳	⟳
Personal Mastery	⟳	⟳	⟳	⟳	⟳		⟳			⟳	⟳		⟳			⟳			⟳		
Team Learning			⟳		⟳	⟳		⟳	⟳			⟳		⟳	⟳		⟳	⟳			⟳
Shared Vision							⟳	⟳	⟳	⟳	⟳	⟳									
Systems Thinking										⟳						⟳	⟳		⟳	⟳	⟳
LEADERSHIP																					
The practice and culture of						⟳															
Finding purpose, values										⟳											
Acting on vision ("walking the talk")									⟳		⟳	⟳									
Aligning resources													⟳			⟳		⟳			
Unlocking potential																		⟳	⟳		
Creating and using leverage								⟳				⟳					⟳	⟳			
Coaching; mentoring						⟳			⟳								⟳				
Harnessing forces of change											⟳									⟳	⟳
MANAGEMENT																					
Setting priorities; planning							⟳			⟳				⟳							⟳

Allocating resources; implementation	
Delegating; empowering	
Living with stress, chaos, uncertainty, "loss" of control	
Creating "balance" (eg. home/work)	

TEAMWORK & COLLABORATION

Building teams and alliances	
Creating commitment	
Creating trust	
Reconciling views	
Dealing with "turf"	
Creating "win-win" situations	
Saying "No"	
Maintaining integrity, values, intention	

CREATIVITY; LEARNING; SHIFTING PARADIGMS

Accessing creativity	
Discovering options	
Working smarter versus harder	

Foreword

Recently, a young Chinese woman told me that one reason *The Fifth Discipline* has become a nonfiction bestseller in China and Taiwan is that "We do not see it as a business book. We see it as a book for personal development." In the five years since the first edition was released in the United States, no one has ever made that comment to me.

By contrast to the young Chinese woman, readers in the United States and Europe seem to struggle with the core of *The Fifth Discipline:* The idea that significant changes in an organization's capacities to learn will only occur when deep changes in how people think and interact occur. We seem to have found a way to disassociate our personal growth and change from the necessary growth and changes in our organizations. We seem somehow to regard the needed changes in organizational structure, reengineering, new strategic alliances, and new technologies as being "out there," rather than "in here."

The result is that few efforts to produce significant organizational change succeed. Frustrated CEOs discover again and again that it is easier to change traditional organizational structures than traditional mental models. For example, an organization can be reengineered, in principle, in terms of "lateral processes" that integrate across traditional functional boundaries, but the same old people in a new organizational structure often produce the same old results. People have spent their lives learning how to look "up and down," not "side to side," waiting for directions from on high, working to climb the corporate ladder, and giving orders to those below. "Reengineering efforts flop more often than they succeed," according to Thomas Kiely in the March/April *1995 Harvard Business Review.* Earlier studies by Ernst and Young and Arthur D. Little found that less than one third of corporate total quality programs started in the late 1980s and early 1990s had significant impacts on profitability and a large fraction were discontinued within a couple of years. Successful change efforts are, if anything, even rarer outside of business environments, in industries such as health care and public education. We seem somehow to think we can get organizational change without personal change and, at least when the changes we seek are deep, we end up getting neither.

The only thing that is surprising about any of this is why it should surprise us. Why should a new "reengineered" organizational structure change reductionistic thinkers into system thinkers? Why should top management mandates lead to the openness and trust needed to build truly shared visions or challenge traditional mental models? Sincere efforts by top managers to foster significant cultural changes have consistently failed for years, subverted by the same authoritarian mindsets, internal politics, and gamesplaying that sapped the energy and commitment in the "old culture." What is truly puzzling is why we should persist in disassociating organizational change and personal change.

Perhaps, the resolution of the puzzle lies in recognizing that this is but one of many symptoms of fragmentation that permeate our lives. Everywhere, we seem to live lives of disconnected pieces: manager and parent, professional self and private self, work and play, analyst and artist, head and heart. This fragmentation is so pervasive that we take it for granted. And we don't even know that we take it for granted. We have so few models of integration—people who bring all of themselves to their work, who parent and manage as one and the same person, who think with their hearts and feel with their minds—that we easily come to believe that such lives are impossible.

I am beginning to think that these domains of fragmentation grow on themselves—much like the progressive branches that form as a tree grows. If this is so, there may be some leverage in pondering some of the earliest fragmentations that develop in our lives as they could shed light on subsequent fragmentations. If we could begin to reverse them, to reintegrate "near the base of the tree," we might naturally foster reintegration at subsequent branches.

In this spirit, Andy Bryner and Dawna Markova's radical proposition that we professionals need to relearn what it means to "learn in our bodies" might seem just a little less radical. Their premise is simple—that we have all been brainwashed by a cultural myth that "learning occurs in our heads" not in all of us, and that, until we challenge that belief, our capacities for any sort of deep learning are severely limited. More importantly, Andy and Dawna do not just preach this message, they offer a concise and well-tested series of physical practices to start on a path of reintegrating the mind and body, by focusing on the most common challenges that professionals of all sorts face in today's workplaces.

For over two years now, we have used these "embodiment practices" that we have learned from Andy and Dawna with managers in programs at the Center for Organizational Learning at MIT. At first, some regard these practices as "the exercise part of the program," much like Oriental aerobics. Some avoid them because they don't want to look awkward. Some trivialize them: "When are we going to get to the real stuff we came here for?" And some actually participate.

All these people then begin to make interesting discoveries. They discover where in their bodies they first experience what their mind calls "stress," how their bodies stiffen, how their breathing becomes shallower. They discover how it feels physically when they are depending on someone else, or have someone depending on them. They discover how they instinctively compensate when they encounter difficulty by exerting more physical effort to get through a situation. These initial discoveries begin to open doors. All of a sudden, a conflictual situation becomes a subject of curiosity: "How does my body give me early warning signals that my mind is about to go into "fight or flight?" People begin to explore how quickly they lose their "centeredness" when they think someone is about to let them down, and then learn how they can maintain that "centeredness." They discover the extraordinary power of "active relaxation" and "gentle focus," with which they can produce results far beyond what is possible with simple physical exertion. They start to see how increased physical awareness can accelerate learning, and how anchoring a new understanding "physically" can make it more accessible in the future.

Gradually the participants rediscover that our physical bodies are an extraordinary instrument for learning. For some this is a profound rediscovery. "Of all the stuff I learned about systems thinking and mental models," wrote a head of Research and Development at a large telecommunications company after a five-day introductory course, "nothing was so directly useful to me as discovering what happens in my body at a meeting."

I do not think infants distinguish what they are learning in their bodies from what they are learning in their heads. Somehow, as we get older, the culture of classrooms, training sessions, and business meetings teaches us a different view of learning. We memorize disconnected facts and digest abstract theories. We can recite what we have "learned" at the latest seminar, but cannot necessarily do anything differently, particularly in real life situations where there is conflict and pressure to perform. Our learning is "in our head" but we don't seem to be able to get it out.

This book shed important light on why we Westerners have so much trouble with the concept of discipline and with the need for committed personal change as a foundation for enduring organizational change. Insofar as we disassociate our learning from our body, we can disassociate our bodies from our work. It is only one small step from there to conclude that all the changes needed are "out there," rather than "out there" and "in here."

If you rise early and walk in any Chinese city, you will see large numbers of people of all ages in the city parks practicing tai chi, one of China's ancient forms of mind-body integration. Their slow, graceful movements are a powerful contrast to the helter-skelter of daily life in most modern organizations. Could it be that the organizations that will thrive in the twenty-first century will be those who achieve this same sort of capacity for continuous, graceful movement; for responsiveness without losing their centeredness?

It is too early to say how far the introductory embodiment practices like those presented in this book can go in establishing a foundation for more learningful organizations, but I believe they are one step in the right direction. Reintegrating mind and body will, I believe, be a vital step in reintegrating work and self, and organizational change and personal change.

—Peter M. Senge
July, 1995

What is the intelligence we're not using that can help us change the way we're thinking about our most pressing challenges?

AN OPENING

Discovering Our Unused Intelligence

"Mr. Duffy lived a short distance from his body."
JAMES JOYCE

The practice hall or "dojo" was in a metal Quonset hut on the edge of a baseball field where the local Little League was having a game. The screaming of kids dissolved as Andy and I walked into the immense fluorescently lit room. The class members sat on their knees on the bright blue mats that covered the floor. As if by some secret signal, they bowed to the teacher or *Sensei,* who then bowed to them. He was Japanese, perhaps fifty, perhaps seventy; there was no way to tell. He wore a white tunic and long black skirt-like pants or *hakama,* the garb of an Aikido master.

A half-dozen burly men circled him menacingly. As they began to close in on him, he was absolutely still, calm, poised, a sea gull nestled in the trough of a tumultuous wave during a hurricane. Suddenly, with shouts that reverberated off the metal walls, they attacked him in unison.

What happened then was remarkable. The master seemed to flow like water into their mass, swirling between them, his black skirt surrounding them. Each time they reached to strike his body, he was not there. As a gyroscope spins faster and faster its motion appears still. So it was with the sensei as he met, diverted, and redirected the energy of his attackers. Projecting them one by one out of the melee, he seemed to lay each down on the ground protectively.

His actions were so effortless that we knew there was something below the surface which could not be readily seen, something unexplained. Whatever it was drew us back the next evening to watch him teach a children's class of five- and six-year-olds. Twenty pair of little rubber flip-flops were neatly lined up on the edge of the mats. The sensei bowed to the children with the same respect he had in the master class the night before. Twenty white garbed boys and girls bent over their knees in unison, bowing back.

The sensei asked Andy to come up and help him demonstrate one of the basic principles of Ki-Aikido—coordination of mind and body. Slightly bemused, Andy stood next to the sensei, whose head barely reached his shoulder. He asked Andy to lift him off the ground. Since he outweighed the master by seventy-five pounds, when he grabbed him around the midsection, the expectation was that he would be able to do it easily. Andy heaved and heaved and heaved. The children put their hands over their mouths, giggling. Andy, who was a wrestler and is still built like one, heaved once again, grunting. There could be no doubt he was trying to the limit of his capacities. The sensei looked at him with those soft, curious brown eyes and stayed firmly planted on the ground, not budging an inch.

After they bowed to each other, the sensei said in a thickly accented and lyrical voice, "When your body and mind are coordinated with the natural energy of the universe, size and force mean nothing at all." Pausing he looked at each child who nodded alertly. "Andy can not fight with me, because I do not need to oppose him. Your power is that of mountains, rivers, the universe. A jellyfish does not have to be strong—it is powered by the whole ocean. Aikido teaches us to bring opposing forces into harmony." It did not seem possible that young children could understand such a vast concept, but when he clapped his hands, they scrambled to their feet. As he went from one to the other, slipping his hands around their midsections, he heaved and grunted, but not one of them budged. All of them, however, smiled proudly, lighting up as if they had swallowed the moon.

After class was over, I approached him rather sheepishly, keeping a respectful distance. When he turned to face me, I felt every molecule of his attention surround me. I was only going to thank him, but my curiosity got the best of me. I had to ask one question. "Excuse me, sensei, but how long did it take you to learn to do that—what you did last night with those men, I mean?"

His eyes shifted slightly to the right and down and the corners of his mouth lifted ever so slightly before he answered. "You mean the *rondori?* The multiple attack?"

"Sure, if that's what you call it. You made it look so simple!"

His students were lining up, waiting to perform the closing class ritual, but he was completely undistracted, totally present with me and my question.

"I have been practicing *rondori* for forty years, but I am sorry, I have not learned it yet. Still, I practice. That's all there is. Simple. Practice. Like life, yes?" He bowed, turned, and was simply and completely gone.

Forty years. Forty years of simple.

THE CHALLENGE TO DISCOVER OUR UNUSED INTELLIGENCE

The multiple challenges of a *rondori*, with its chaotic forces closing in rapidly from many different directions, would seem familiar to any person in a position of leadership today. What was there below the surface that could not be readily seen that enabled the sensei to respond in a way so unlike most of us? How did he manage to remain balanced, calm, and simultaneously connected to himself and others?

He gave a clue the next night in the demonstration of mind and body alignment. Because he was internally integrated mentally, physically, and spiritually, he couldn't be fragmented or distracted by the pull of outside forces. He had been practicing an "intelligence" for forty years, an innately natural way of learning.

The sensei's fluidity and grace under pressure, the unified presence of his attention—essential elements of what is currently being demanded of leaders—can not be learned from listening to lectures for forty years or watching video tapes. His learning was embodied, continually being integrated "on the mat" and in his life.

Like the sensei, others in sports and the martial, healing, and performing arts know that the development of capacities to a remarkable level requires the practice of integration of mind, body, and spirit. What would it mean for organizational leaders then, to integrate their physical and mental intelligences, to practice their profession rather than simply do a job?

Anyone in organizational life is fully aware that we stand at a turning point. We can no longer think new thoughts in the same old ways. Thinking together about the future and our part in it will depend on our ability to learn to respond and interact in new, flexible, and inquiring ways. Peter Senge has stated that "the most leverage occurs where we have the least awareness." In terms of our thinking processes and productive capability, the area of least awareness is our physical bodies. We have neglected our ability to think physically, to think on our feet.

What is it that keeps pulling us further away from our physical selves, particularly at work? How is it that "successful" people can live their whole lives, accomplishing many things, and discover at the age of sixty-two that they're on death's doorstep? How do we begin to close the gap between where we live—the locus of our experience—and our awareness of our

"Every living thing reflects an intelligence that the human intellect cannot index or adequately explain and therefore cannot be taught from an external source."
J. ALLEN BOONE

physical intelligence? What would it take for us to appreciate the Aikido statement that the body is the weather vane of the mind?

THERE'S A LITTLE OF MR. DUFFY IN ALL OF US

"If your learning isn't in your body," asks Peter Senge, "then where is it?" Most of us tend to think it happens just in our heads. Growing evidence suggests, however, that for learning to be complete and usable, it must include the following components: auditory or words, visual or pictures, and kinesthetic or physical experience. Most existing learning methods include verbal language and visual imagery, but omit physical experience. For some people, even an initial understanding of a concept does not occur until they have that body experience. It is generally becoming accepted that people learn in different ways. For some, kinesthetic learning helps to organize experience. For others, it is a means to sort out different possibilities. For still others, it stimulates the generation of new ideas.

Thinking through our bodies can go a long way toward facilitating the kinds of flexible, creative minds so desperately needed in organizations today. The word "incorporated" gives us this clue in its etymology; it's Latin root *corporare,* means to adopt or form into a body. Incorporating or embodying our business thinking is a dynamic way to explore the path between abstract ideas and implemented action.

In our Western culture, the problem-solving potential of our bodies has been virtually untapped. This phenomenon is due, to a large extent, to our educational history. Early on, kinesthetic or body experience was relegated to gym class, sports, shop, and home economics. On the job, our bodies are sometimes

"The illiterate of the year 2000 will not be the individual who cannot read and write, but the one who cannot learn, unlearn and relearn."
ALVIN TOFFLER

just one more project to be kept groomed, healthy, dependable, and conditioned to contribute to production needs. We have been trained in time management, in negotiation, in quality procedures and measurement, but we have never been taught to notice how we are relating physically or energetically to the content, people, and events of our jobs.

"Learning that is not conducted through a new way of action is not learning. Learning is a crystallization of experience."
MOSHE FELDENKRAIS

At work, this inexperience with physical thinking places us at the mercy of unexamined responses: stances of control, reactivity, rigidity, and opposition. These ingrained ways of thinking predictably result in stress, conflict, and wasted human potential. All too often we address complex and difficult issues by simply paying attention to ideas, rather than also noticing what is physically going on between people in the moment. For example, if someone were standing across from you saying, "I really want to understand what you mean," but his or her hands are clenched into fists, jaw and neck muscles tensed, breath shallow, your response might be very different than if he or she stood next to you, smiling, one hand on your shoulder, with a relaxed smile on his or her face. The words would be the same, but the interaction would totally change the meaning of the message you received.

Our bodies are receptive to so many more languages than words. Work pressure and disagreement are often felt as tension in the body and expressed as verbal defensiveness or rigidity. Learning through the body directly can soften our certainties, and open our minds in curiosity. Including the physical dimension of reality as a vehicle for learning can help us access a wisdom that most business settings completely overlook. Physical thinking invites us to develop an awareness of our bodies from the inside out, reconnecting to a natural source of vitality and generativity.

It is essential in these times of rapid change to anchor our learnings physically, to integrate them by embodying them. In this way, we can, like the sensei, develop flexible thinking which can generate fresh responses to old problems and help us find balance in the midst of confusion.

In our consulting work with organizations, we discovered a void in which people were facing immense pressure to change with no idea of how to support and learn with each other at an individual level. With the encouragement of Peter Senge, Fred Kofman, and others at MIT's Organizational Learning Center at MIT, we begin presenting these practices for physical thinking as part of programs on organizational learning to companies like EDS, Phillips, Shell, and Chrysler. Participants who began with lukewarm amusement ended up teaching the practices enthusiastically to their colleagues. More and more we were met with the question, "Where can we get more of this stuff?" *An Unused Intelligence* is our response to that question.

We started the research for this book by asking managers and CEOs from the above companies and others such as Ford, U.S. West, AT&T, Merck, Armco, Harley Davidson, and Intel, "What are the most challenging questions you face doing business today?" The most common responses were:

1. What are the new ways of thinking we need in order to implement the essential ideas of a learning organization?

2. How do you manage job stress and change the ways of thinking that contribute to it?

3. How do we create trust and support on the job when everything keeps changing?

4. How do we establish mutual respect for diverse needs in the workplace?

"Each of us is something of a schizophrenic personality, tragically divided against ourselves."
MARTIN LUTHER KING, JR.

"All things
are ready if our
minds be so."
WILLIAM
SHAKESPEARE

5. How do you find your intention and move forward in the distraction of daily challenges?

6. How do you deal with impasses between coworkers?

7. How do we get more effective results using fewer resources?

8. How do we learn to perceive the whole instead of just thinking about how we can survive individually?

These questions became the center of gravity for this book's nine chapters of practice and inquiry. Our purpose is to share some of what we've learned, both from our personal practice and from our work with professionals in business, health care, and educational organizations. It is our hope that it will contribute to your closing that short distance between where you live and your body.

1

What are the new ways of thinking we need to implement the essential ideas of a learning organization?

PHYSICAL THINKING

Learning to Change Our Organizational Mind

"The significant problems we face cannot be solved at the same level of thinking we were at when we created them."
ALBERT EINSTEIN

NUMMY AND DUMMY

From Dawna:

Andy and I came to physical thinking from opposite paths. The first thing I noticed about him was how completely he lived in his body—he reeked of health and athletic shoes. He was always moving, wanting to do things and feel things. He described himself as a man of action and few words. When we first met, I affectionately called him "Dummy." He appropriately called me "Nummy," because I lived everywhere except my body. As far as I was concerned for most of my life, my body was a limousine for my brain. Maybe a pedestal would be a more appropriate metaphor.

Movement was not part of my picture. I was a vision vamp, an idea idol. I flunked every physical education course in college except for modern dance, which required only the ability to roll around on the floor. Whenever I watched physical activity of any kind, I translated what I saw immediately into a metaphor or analogy: A football game to me was merely a bunch of men enacting the struggle of two corporations for market dominance. A run down a ski trail represented how a person could maneuver through life's obstacles.

When Andy and I first met, I was struggling with what had been diagnosed as a case of terminal cancer. Up until that point, I experienced my body as fifty-five percent pain and forty-five percent Styrofoam. All the best medical "brains" I could find had given up on it. I was the Dummy now, left on my own to try to decipher the language my body was speaking. I was a "stranger in a strange land," but since Andy lived in this corporal territory, I assumed he could help me with the translation.

At the same time, I began to study the work of a man named Moshe Feldenkrais, an Israeli physicist and black belt

"Driven by the force of love, the fragments of the world seek each other that the world may come into being."
TEILHARD DE CHARDIN

judo practitioner, who pioneered a receptive, collaborative form of body work called "psycho-physical re-education." When I first heard of it, what intrigued me was that it was an approach that involved learning, not fixing. Re-education between my mind and body was definitely what my healing required.

Moshe was a shortish, balding, intense man who looked nothing like any gym teacher I had ever had. I walked into my first class with him in Berkeley, hearing a familiar internal voice in my mind: "Why am I doing this? I'll never be able to do these exercises. I'll just make a fool of myself once again. Maybe I could hide in the ladies room until the coffee break." But learning to integrate my mind and body was a life-or-death matter for me at that point, and this man was touted as a genius in the field. So I lay down on the floor with the other eighty or so people and promised myself I'd really try hard to do this physical stuff right.

But "right" was not what this "stuff" was about. The movements Moshe and his assistants talked us through were so simple, even "Klara Klutz" could do them. Feldenkrais taught that where there was little awareness, there was more likely to be injury or disease in the body due to decreased circulation. Conversely with an increase in awareness, there would be increased circulation and thus more potential for health. We were encouraged again and again to "underwhelm" ourselves, to do less than we could do, but enjoy it more, to increase our sensate awareness of each movement. This "awareness" was something brand new to me. And magical. With it, sensation flooded back into my long-numbed body. There didn't seem to be any way to do these movements "wrong." It was like a bad joke turned good. Being dumb was helping me not be numb. I began to understand that my body was thinking in its own way, with its own kind of logic. I didn't accumulate ideas, but I did experience the sweet simplicity that can exist in every moment of reality.

As time went on, Andy and I created a learning/teaching partnership and began to study Ki-Aikido together. Klara Klutz came to every class. Where Andy would immediately understand and perform every *waza* (physical form) we were taught, I would stumble and bumble and do my best not to put out someone's eye with my elbow. While learning and remembering the kinesthetic details of the movements was still slow, I felt every movement, and enjoyed every fall. I always left class in a semi-rapturous state with my mind spinning analogies for the organizational world where we were working. "Oh, of course! That double arm-pull is just like how we learn to deal with the either-or decisions that re-engineering is bringing us every day!" I found myself in old situations, such as confrontational meetings, where I was about to rigidly defend my point of view, and suddenly an Aikido move would flash across the screen of my mind, and I would respond in a much more flexible and centered way.

Now when Andy and I bring this way of thinking to organizations, we find some people who immediately feel at home with it, as if they are speaking a native tongue. Others join Klara in the back of the room, wondering if it will help them lose weight.

Since this channel of learning is largely untutored, it is also largely uncontaminated and free of assumptions. Those who don't think they can peel a banana in a coordinated fashion, are often the most surprised and delighted by the innovative thinking that is stimulated by learning in this way. Unconscious assumptions become conscious in a way that is serious fun.

"Am I the bulb or the light?"
JOSEPH CAMPBELL

People begin to think on their feet and walk their talk in a way that is completely involving. But it does take patience with the unknown and unfamiliar. As with the stars, it's sometimes hard to see clearly until we adjust to the dark.

From Andy:

On the 9th grade wrestling mat for the first time in my life, I realized I was good at something. It was a milestone moment, distinguished by a sweet feeling, the joy of being alive.

In subsequent years, other such moments occurred on wooded ski slopes in New York; on an oil-drilling rig in Pennsylvania; on sheer rock faces and glaciers while studying and teaching at Colorado Outward Bound and Wyoming's National Outdoor Leadership School; 50 feet up on top of a framed house while working as a builder in New Hampshire; on my motorcycle in Vermont commuting to work with U.S. Olympic Skiers as a massage therapist and chiropractic assistant; on a windsurfer flying across the ocean in the Dry Tortugas. In all of them, I was fully alive, thinking in and through my body.

Mysteriously, my school experiences and jobs were devoid of these kind of moments. I was taught to work very hard to look good, to get good grades so I could get into a good MBA program at Dartmouth so I could then get a good banking job in NYC so I would then have good references on my resumé. But all that was "good," according to the standards of the outside world, left me feeling phony and lonely. I was living like a fish out of water or a mind out of body.

And then, my life brought me an important teacher in the improbable form of Dawna. She introduced me to what she had been learning in her own healing process. She did what

"We are all strangers in a strange land longing for home, but not quite knowing where home is. We glimpse it sometimes in our dreams or as we turn a corner and suddenly there is a strange sweet familiarity that vanishes almost as soon as it comes."
MADELEINE L'ENGLE

seemed at the time, weird and wonderful things such as ask me to describe a problem with my hands, without words. She also asked me disturbing questions such as, "Why do you spend so much of your time doing things that don't bring you joy?"

We began to study a martial art called Shin Shin Toitsu Ki Aikido, which means the harmony of mind and body with spirit. We had heard about Aikido from a friend, Terry Dobson, who studied in Japan with the founder, Morihei Ueshiba.

In my first class with Sensei Richard Kuboyama in Hawaii, I did what I knew best—used all my strength to be as good as possible at what I was doing. The sensei told me to stop using strength, to relax, to not try so hard. I had never heard a man say anything like this. He told me to be easy and natural in the face of strong energy. These concepts were so foreign to my wrestling and football and work ethic that he could have been speaking Martian. Over and over again I did what I had been trained to do and "strong-armed" my practice partners. I explained to him that for years I had been taught to "Kick the competitions' butt," or "Do some damage." He just smiled patiently and went on teaching me about a different kind of power.

I came to understand the rigidity and limitations of the kind of strength I had been most proud of. One night in the class, he told me, "Even if you are strong enough to defeat a muscular opponent who weighs 400 pounds, there will come a day when you meet a 401-pound opponent, and your strength will be defeated. To influence another, you must learn to work in harmony with their energy instead of struggling against it." At forty, I was coming to understand the wisdom of this.

The founder of this philosophy, Morihei Ueshiba, was a great warrior in the samurai "budo" tradition. And then came the bombings at Nagasaki and Hiroshima, and with them, the ulti-

"It's not about lack of action. It's about having action come from a quiet place inside."
RAM DASS

mate realization that no one wins a war. As his life and practice evolved, his teachings redefined the concepts of warrior, and winning and losing. He developed an art that did not focus on injuring the attacker, but rather flowing with the energy while avoiding harm.

Ueshiba's Aikido taught a physical discipline and a way of life, the essence of which was to respond powerfully and influence others through the mastery of oneself. At the end of his life, he realized that a "fighting mind" only attracts fights. His final definition of the mission of Aikido was, "the realization of love."

Having the physical experience of a third option beyond fight or flight, and win or lose, opened my mind to a world of new possibilities. I found the principles immensely useful because they are natural laws of the mind, body, and spirit, which apply to all aspects of life. Dawna and I combined our thirty-five years of service in the health and educational fields to develop a mind-body-spirit synthesis for learning.

IS THIS ANY OF YOUR BUSINESS?

Sixty-five percent of the companies listed in the 1970 Fortune 500 are no longer in existence. Obviously, the way we defined and achieved success in the past, is no longer effective. The "Knowledge Era" is radically changing our understanding of what represents value in an organizational context. In the June 1995 cover story, *Fortune* magazine described intellectual capital as America's most valuable asset: "The challenge is to find what you have—and use it!" This means unleashing our capacity to learn individually and together.

By awakening to the importance of expanding intellectual

capital—our collective ability to think flexibly and learn within our organizations—as much as we do structural capital, we can revitalize our organizations.

"If people are assets, why do we treat them like expenses?" challenges Daniel Kim of the Organizational Learning Center at MIT, and cofounder of the Systems Thinker. "On the balance sheet, they appear as payroll liabilities. If people are really a company's most valuable asset, it is strange we do so little to keep track of, understand, and benefit from their full capabilities. If we really treated employees as assets, they would not be seen as expenses to be cut out, but assets in which we would invest and expect to get a return." The long-term prosperity of organizations will depend, to a large extent, on management's ability to leverage these "hidden" values, as well as the company's ability to learn and adapt as fast as the market changes.

Few people in organizations today feel their world is any more stable and predictable than it was ten years ago. Few expect it to become more predictable in the future. We seem to be living in a world of rapid and turbulent change, a world of what author Peter Vaill calls "permanent white water," where we can barely catch our breath as we maneuver from one crisis to another. Is there a middle ground between traditional bureaucratic organizations with their difficulty adapting to change and total unpredictable chaos? Is there something between blind defensiveness and pure reactiveness?

In Aikido, instead of resisting or fighting against the forces around you, you respond by putting yourself in a position so that no energy is lost to friction or opposition. All of your attention is focused on learning and creating positive action.

It is unlikely that organizations will develop a capacity for

"We have a lot of infrastructure in our organization for decision making; we have very little infrastructure for learning."
BOB ALLEN, Chairman of AT&T

flexible responsiveness without the individuals in that organization developing that capacity. We will not achieve this through management edicts, new incentive systems, or reorganization. We will only achieve this when we learn how to learn—together.

With more responsibility and less certainty than ever before, we need to be able to live in the question, rather than drive for the answers. How do we move from a culture of certainty to a culture of inquiry? In the shifting markets of the fast-moving "New Economy," an aptitude for continued learning has become a mission-critical skill for both individuals and organizations.

Thus, there has recently grown a worldwide interest in how business, healthcare, and educational organizations can become learning organizations—organizations whose central essence has to do with learning rather than controlling, and with building new knowledge rather than blindly living out of the concepts and routines of the past.

In doing research for this book, we searched for ways to create these collective fields of inquiry. We looked for tools that could be used to build a bridge between unanswerable questions and the wisdom that exists within and between the stakeholders of any given system. We looked for processes that would dissolve the walls between what one intuitively knows and what one most needs to know. We attempted to find an approach that would stimulate people within an organization to think in more flexible ways.

"I am never defeated, however fast the enemy may attack. It is not because my technique is faster. It is not a question of speed. The fight is finished before it is begun. Winning means winning over the mind of discord in yourself. It is to accomplish your bestowed mission."
MORIHEI UESHIBA, O SENSEI

THE FIVE DISCIPLINES OF A LEARNING ORGANIZATION

One particular approach to developing learning organizations that has gained international attention because it seeks to integrate the need for both organizational and individual change is that popularized by Peter Senge, of the Organizational Learning Center at MIT. With its set of principles and practices, it creates a dynamic context for both individual and collective learning. Senge says, "Through learning, we re-perceive the world and our relationship to it. A learning organization is a place where people are continually discovering how they create their reality and how they can change it" (1994).

The core of establishing a learning organization can be found in what Senge calls the five disciplines or lifelong programs of study and practice: Personal Mastery, Team Learning, Mental Models, Shared Vision, and Systems Thinking. Senge describes these concepts in detail in *The Fifth Discipline* and, with Charlotte Roberts, Richard Ross, Bryan Smith, and Art Kleiner, in a pragmatic guide to their application entitled *The Fifth Discipline Fieldbook* (1995). Senge's five-discipline theory defines the overall territory that this book seeks to explore. Some readers will be familiar with the five disciplines, but for those who aren't, we included an Appendix that briefly summarizes them and a matrix of their interrelationships with the practices in this book.

With regard to the disciplines, Senge says that, "at some level, there is nothing new in them. They represent modern articulations of very old ideas—ideas like vision, dialogue, and the understanding systems—along with new tools and methods for practicing the disciplines in practical managerial settings."

There are many other tools within the expanding knowledge of learning organizations to help people examine their

> *"The manager of the future will merely be a learning guide."*
> PETER DRUCKER

assumptions and explore their mental models—systems dynamics, strategic dialogue, computer learning labs—just to name a few. But people struggle with how to put the five disciplines into practice on a daily basis. We keep hearing, "I agree completely with these ideas, but how do we put them into practice on Monday morning?" We believe this struggle will continue until the disciplines become more integrated into physical awareness.

That is because no learning is really yours until it is in your body. You need to have a hologram for a reference point, and this occurs only with a cellular experience. When people ask, "How do we *do* these ideas?" they are asking for a kinesthetic component to their learning. Thus to assimilate concepts completely so we can utilize them as needed, we must be able to access the physical intelligence that corresponds to those ideas. This book is designed to enhance your implementation of them.

Mental Models:

In this book your awareness of mental models will expand through the practice of centering, as you'll learn in chapter 2. In addition, each time you shift from examining an idea to contemplating a physical thinking practice of that idea, you will be increasing the elasticity of your mental models. The integration questions after each practice are designed to help you do just that.

Personal Mastery:

Each of the chapters in this book includes a "solo" practice, which is designed to help you increase the clarity with which you perceive your current reality, as well as your personal vision, and become more comfortable in the creative tension with which you hold them both.

Team Learning:

The group practices in each chapter are designed to foster relational logic and to provide you and your associates with opportunities to develop the possibility of achieving a collaborative advantage.

Shared Vision:

What happens when we shift a guiding image? How do we do it? What core processes help this shift? By experiencing and processing the practices in this book with others in your work setting, shared vision will begin to emerge naturally. In chapter five you will find yourself talking much more deeply about the things that have meaning to you individually and as a community.

Systems Thinking:

There are several ways of approaching Systems Thinking—as a philosophical base for one's life, as a collection of learning processes to address any given problem, and as stories or case studies to illustrate specific situations. Chapter eight focuses particularly on one approach to perceiving the whole, while the paired practices in each chapter help you perceive the possibilities that exist in relational thinking.

LEARNING TO LEARN—CORPORATELY

How much learning actually goes on in business? "As a society, we tend to confuse learning with training. We naturally look to training professionals to make learning happen, just as we used to look to teachers to make it happen when we were children. In fact, learning is a much more complex phenomenon than can ever be limited to the classroom," Peter Senge stated in the

"It has been said that if you don't have discipline, it is like trying to walk without legs."
CHOGYAM
TRUNGPA

keynote speech of a recent conference on organizational learning. "It [learning] is inextricably connected to the way we live our lives, and to the excitement, challenges, motivation, and support woven throughout our daily experience."

We have been trained to climb the ladders of success using logical thinking to solve problems and binary thinking to make decisions. We have been trained to eliminate all possibilities as soon as we can in order to come up with the right answer. We are then promoted and given a prize—a high score on an examination, a degree, or a higher salary. We have been trained to sort information in two categories, as if it were laundry: clean or dirty, white or colored, valuable or useless. Then we stand between the two and choose the "right" one.

We create what David Issacs of Whole Systems Associates calls "expertocracies"—structures of learning based on the linear ladder or the binary see-saw. Either I know or I don't know. You know more than I do, so you're "one-up." You have more and I have less. Based on this, I am less smart and therefore I am one-down. But, in fact, this is about information accumulation, not learning. It is based on the assumption that what we need to learn is always external to ourselves, that who we are equals what we know, and that our ability to acquire knowledge is fixed, limited, and predetermined by circumstances beyond our control.

Nothing is further from the truth. In fact, the human brain is unsurpassed as a learning mechanism. It can distinguish and store, on the average, three hundred thousand different voice tones, two million shades of color. The sophistication of our capacity is literally astronomical—we have the same number of neurons in our central nervous system as there are stars in the galaxy—one hundred billion. It takes one-fiftieth of a second for a message to get from your brain to your foot. The memory capacity of this system is almost infinite.

But having this capacity and using it are two different matters. We have been carefully trained in school and the workplace never to risk making a mistake. We learn by sitting still and waiting for instructions on how to do it right and solve problems by coming up with the one right answer. We spend our time and interest on what gets done, not on the overall process of doing it. We are well trained, but how much do we allow ourselves to learn?

Learning is a very different process than training. The brain is like a cybernetic mechanism, such as a heat-seeking device or a thermostat. It functions most effectively when it knows its goal and receives clear feedback from the inner and outer environment that helps it make a series of ever-decreasing adjustments. True learning then is automatic and inevitable, like a child learning to crawl, walk, reach for a cup, or speak with no instructions at all.

Here's an opportunity to try your first experiment in physical thinking to experience this idea in an embodied way. All that's required is your curiosity:

"The purpose of today's learning is to defeat yesterday's understanding."
MIYAMOTO MUSASHI

Stand on one foot and be curious about the minute adjustments that your body automatically makes to keep you in balance. The wobbles become even smaller as your body-mind system experiments with possibilities and becomes aware of when it is off-course by responding to feedback.

Just for the sake of experimentation, try balancing on the other leg, but this time instruct yourself as you do it: "No that's wrong. You're doing too much of . . . not enough of. . . ." Emphasize to yourself what you are doing wrong.

Having lived through both of these options, please reflect on the following questions, drawing on your own embodied experience rather than an "idea" of what you assume will be the "right" answer: Which way was your learning more effective? Which way was it more enjoyable? Which way motivated you to want to do more?

How we learn, by and large, determines what we learn. Performance is optimized when the brain remembers its successes and discards its failures without berating itself or becoming full of self-congratulation, when it leaves behind ingrained instructions on how to "do it right."

THE CORPORATE ASSETS OF EMBODIED LEARNING

We believe there are at least two reasons why embodied learning is so powerful. The first is that it helps us change the context in which we are thinking about something. Milton Erickson, M.D., who was one of the greatest clinicians in the field of unconscious learning, explained that adult learning was very difficult if you begin at the level of the rational belief system. His research and experience indicated, rather, that if you changed the context in which a person is thinking about something, his or her perceptions would change. This enables the learner to change his or her behavior, which then makes changing beliefs possible: change the context, change the perception, change the behavior, change the belief. Erickson said that when most people reverse the order, they get stuck in habitual mental ruts.

Here's an example: When we were coaching a company executive recently, he described a manager who had been "driving him crazy" for years. He said he felt totally ineffective getting through to him. We asked him what internal resource he had that helped connect with other managers in difficult situations. He replied immediately that it was his sense of humor. When asked what metaphor he would use to describe the person he was having trouble with, he responded flippantly, "A Venus-flytrap."

So we called a local garden supply center and had a Venus-flytrap sent to his office, suggesting he learn as much as he could about its care and feeding. For the next year, whenever the manager entered his office, the senior executive looked at the plant, sat quietly for a moment, and found himself perceiving the "troublemaker" in a whole new way. He came to believe that the manager was someone who was hungry to do well, instead of a troublemaker. By changing the context to a plant, he changed the way he was perceiving, and could open his mind to many more possibilities of response.

Howard Gardner, Professor of Education, Harvard University, discovered that most of his top-level graduate students tested poorly in all of the standard measures of understanding—they knew a great many facts but could not apply this information to everyday situations, such as why it gets warmer in the summer in the northern hemisphere. Erickson said that using one's mind powerfully means learning from one's experience, as the executive did with his study of the plant (and the graduate students did not do), and applying it to another situation. Clearly, this is a practice we could all use.

Physical thinking creates a practice field where you can change the context of your questions. It demonstrates how an abstract idea, a difficult question, a conceptual incoherency can manifest in action and interaction. It helps us move from tacit

"People have been learning in an environment that is seventy to ninety percent fear and frustration with ten to thirty percent interest. Our goal is to change the percentage so that interest and curiosity are more than fifty percent of our motivation."
WENDY PALMER, SENSEI

or implicit knowing to the explicit realm where we can perceive the opportunities that were not evident before.

The second reason for the effectiveness of this kind of learning is that it uses the largely untapped resources that exist within our physical being. Over the millennia, nature has encoded much of the wisdom of our species in our bodies, yet we have severely limited ourselves to what author Thomas Berry calls "cultural coding." We have lost the ability to receive and discern the encoded body knowledge. Much of Western culture views the body as an object to be manipulated. Body consciousness has come to mean the external image we project and create with the help of advertising and the local gym. Thus, to rediscover that we belong—to ourselves, our organizations, and our communities—we must first rediscover that we belong in our bodies.

Now let's practice with a paired experiment in physical thinking that's related to one of the disciplines of a learning organization: the aspect of personal mastery that involves living out your vision. You may have read or heard a great deal about this idea. What is it like to "incorporate" it?

Let's imagine you are somebody who is quite clear in his or her intention and purpose at work, but you find yourself getting stopped by one external obstacle after another. Attending each obstruction seems to take most of your energy, leaving you little for moving toward what you really want. You'll need someone to help you with this one.

Stand at one side of a room and imagine what you really want is at the opposite end. Ask your partner to stand midway in between, facing you. Begin to walk toward your destination, and as you pass your partner, he or she extends out an arm across your chest blocking your passage. When this happens, put all your awareness on that arm. Feel familiar?

To practice an alternative, think of how a person splits a log of wood effectively. If you aim at the piece of wood, it's apt to chip. But if you aim at the block on which the log is resting, your ax will go right through the log cleanly. In the same manner, this time walk across the room think forward toward your destination, not against but through your partner's arm. No need to stop or struggle, just think through it. You will move toward your destination with ease. What was an obstacle before becomes just a challenge to help you remember where you really want to go.

Here's the opportunity for you to use your mind in a powerful way. How could you transfer what you just learned back to that similar circumstance at work?

HOW TO USE THIS BOOK

This book does not offer answers to the top questions being asked in business today. To be honest, we don't know those answers (nor do we trust anyone who says he or she does)! Instead, we offer experiential practice fields within which you can inquire into those questions in whole new ways, generating new options of response.

We invite you to develop two aspects of an unused intelligence: the first is the capacity to think physically and the second is the facility for applying this type of thinking to key organizational challenges you are facing today.

All of the physical thinking practices in this book emphasize the following principles:

⑥ developing yourself first before trying to change someone else;

⑥ increasing your awareness of what you are doing habitually;

⑥ coming to know your intention in any given interaction;

"It may be that when we no longer know which way to go we have begun our real journey. The mind that is not baffled is not employed. The impeded stream is the one that sings."
WENDELL BERRY

- turning conflict into a challenge to innovate;
- acting for positive change within the system as a whole;
- presuming collaboration.

Because we believe that different people learn in different ways, we invite you to use this book in the way that is most effective for you. Each chapter contains contextual and conceptual information, and metaphoric learning in the form of stories, physical practices, integration questions, scenarios, and case studies. Some people ask, "What is this about?" before they have any experience. If that is the case with you, you may prefer to read the orientation and conceptual material first. Others prefer a "side door," and want to learn through metaphors and personal stories. For those readers, we suggest beginning with the teaching tale. And then there are readers who ask, "So what?" and "Now what?" right away because they want to have an experience and then consider ideas and stories. If this is how you work best, please feel free to skip over all the other material and start with the practices themselves.

Because the sequence of the book is intentional, try to follow it concurrently with your own learning-style preference in mind. You may prefer, for instance, to read a whole practice and then go back and actually do it. Others may prefer to read the practices into a tape recorder and then let their your own recorded words guide them through step by step.

Please become the author of your own experience. If the presented business cases do not match your own situation, just consider how they relate to your own circumstances, whatever they may be. This book is not about right or wrong. Each practice is a learning mirror which will reveal an infinite number of lessons for each practitioner. Each practice illustrates options of response, some of which will be more effective than others.

By now, you probably understand that if you just read this book and don't do the practices you'll merely accumulate more information, but add very little to your actual learning. Please give yourself the gift of uncovering your own wisdom through practice.

Here are a few further suggestions which should help maximize your learning:

⑤ Practice safely within the comfort zone of your particular physical abilities. This may mean doing less than you are capable of but with more awareness; this may mean pausing and setting limits when you or others are pushing you too far or too fast; this may mean doing the practice in your imagination, if your body cannot do what is suggested; this may mean challenging one another to grow and learn, instead of testing to prove who's right or wrong.

⑤ Create a dignified practice space and time to commit to this learning inquiry. Structure your practice time, whether it be ten minutes or an hour, to be free from outside interruptions and demands. Include in that time periods of reflection, in which you can ponder how the practice is relevant to your daily activity.

⑤ Bring a genuine curiosity or spirit of inquiry. Avoid the cynical "been there, done that" judgmental approach, in which participants go through the motions for a few minutes and conclude with a sarcastic jokes or two. In order to maintain that sense of curiosity, avoid voting on practices as good or bad. There is a lot to gain from practices that seem awkward. Awkwardness is often our way of experiencing our "learning edges." Notice if you need to react to awkwardness defensively. Ask yourself, Is there something important for me here that would make experiencing awkwardness worthwhile?

"If you really want to improve your situation, you can work on the one thing over which you have control— yourself. . . . Expand your perspective by expanding your mind." STEVEN R. COVEY

"As felt, so fashioned." SANSKRIT PROVERB

⑥ Overall, cultivate a respectful learning mindset. These learnings are not like typical gym or aerobic class exercises. They are participatory action research. How can you create a time for such research when it is safe to make mistakes, safe not to know, safe to enjoy your awkwardness, safe to wonder and daydream?

⑥ Choose your practice partners with awareness, intent, and a mutual understanding of how the practice time is to be lived out. Your partners can be from your own functional areas or from cross-functional areas for maximum impact on your organization or team.

NOURISHMENT FOR LIFE

The Swedish phrase: *narings liv* means both "business" and "nourishment for life." The Chinese phrase: *Jo Sang Yi* means both "to do business" and "to do life's meaning with heart." Whatever you call your life force (spirit, *ki*, *chi*, *prana*, God), you will be here for a finite number of years. The average life span in this country is 75 years for men, 79 for women. How will you live out the precious time that you have?

At it's broadest level, this book is about power. It is about spirit. It is about how you explore and act on the callings of your soul. It is about simultaneously benefiting yourself and the world of which you are a part. Whatever your motivation in reading it, we hope you will also discover some additional benefits including serious fun; a closer connection with yourself and others; increased personal satisfaction and joy; increased appreciation of your own competencies and vision; the uncovering of stories about your life that take you beyond fight and struggle; increased wonder about the miracle and mystery of your soul's journey; and a closer connection to the spirit that binds us together.

"Given the right circumstances, from no more than dreams, determination, and the liberty to try, quite ordinary people consistently do extraordinary things."
DEE HOCK

Using the resource of your physical intelligence will call for a new relatedness with your emotions, body, spirit, and with others in the workplace. Through embodied learning, we can come to appreciate the origins of our own and other people's struggles, increase our confidence to trust ourselves, and expand our ability to choose how we respond to any given situation. In teams and groups, it becomes a practice field for collective inquiry, an "incorporated" dialogue that can help us actualize more of what we were meant to be. It provides learning in a subtle but profound way, as if you threw a small pebble into a pond. In and of itself, it may seem to have little substance, but the ripples it creates can spread outward a great distance.

"What can we gain by sailing to the moon if we are not able to cross the abyss that separates us from ourselves?"
THOMAS MERTON

2

IN THE CENTER
OF THE STORM

Shifting
from
Stress
to Balance

*"In times of change, the learners will inherit the earth
while the learned will find themselves beautifully equipped
to deal with a world that no longer exists."*

ERIC HOFFER

IN THE MIDST OF IT ALL

inspired by Thich Nhat Hanh

Imagine you have climbed to the top-most branches of a huge old oak tree. The perspective is quite wonderful from up there as you can see all the way to the horizon. But suddenly things begin to change. You notice a gray thickening in the air, and before you know it, a storm begins to move across the landscape. The winds lash at your cheeks, tear the leaves from the very branches you are clinging to. You hold on for dear life, but all around you, you can hear limbs cracking and breaking. In the chaos of the moment, it seems as if all is lost.

As the storm intensifies, you take a deep breath and loosen your grip. Simultaneously, you allow gravity to pull you down. At first you slip, but in moments you find yourself hugging the thick trunk of the tree, your feet supported by the gnarled roots and the earth under them. Even though the storm rages all around you, the trunk of the tree is solid and unmoving. From this position, you know in the canyons of your bones that the tree is not lost, and thus you can know exactly where you are.

As this story shows, the more pressured the environment, the more valuable it is to be able to shift into a stable, quiet thinking state so you have a centered leverage point from which to make decisions.

We cannot suceed in today's marketplace if we do not learn from our experience. And we cannot learn from our experience if we do not develop habits of reflective action and active reflection. But how do we learn to actually change the way we are thinking, to come to value introspection enough to actually learn new ways to do it?

"Nothing happens without personal transformation."
W. EDWARDS DEMING

ORIENTATION

In a feature story about the need for leaders to acquire skills of reflection, *Fortune* magazine (August 1994) quotes lecturer Richard Pascale as saying, "When you're at the end of your rope, introspection becomes particularly important. The ability to live in the question, rather than drive for the answers helps you keep the antennae up and the eyes open." Mainstream corporations such as AT&T, Pepsi Co., and Aetna are integrating various forms of introspection training into management development programs because they feel it is crucial to their growth.

This subtle shift toward reflection is easier said than done, however. In this culture, if people appear busy doing something, we never disturb them; we wait until they are still and quiet and then we interrupt. In the West, the pressure to be constantly busy starts when we are children. We are told as children to hurry up, stop dawdling, shake a leg, get a move on. If we daydream, which is a reflective state, we are told we need to "pay attention." In Japan, however, the opposite is true; if people are still and quiet, they are assumed to be in a very important state of reflection and therefore not to be interrupted.

Albert Einstein, who certainly developed and utilized a great deal of his intellectual capital, was once heard to muse to a friend that when "daydreaming" he was continually doing "thought experiments," contemplating the effects of placing clocks in various parts of the universe long before he could afford to buy a carriage clock for his own home. Unbeknownst to his teachers, his apparent lack of attention was the way Einstein learned to dream up the theory of relativity! In today's culture, however, he would have been diagnosed with an "attention deficit disorder."

Sometimes not until you are doing nothing does it become apparent how much you are *really* doing, and how tensely you are doing it. By loosening the knots of your will, releasing your clenched grip, taking a moment of time to let time go, you can begin to pay attention in a different, more balanced way. By taking a moment to allow your body and soul to catch up with your mind, you can reconnect and operate from your integrity rather than being blown off course by the winds of change. In the office, this can be as simple as taking three deep breaths before answering the phone—using the source of agitation and distraction as a signal to find your center of gravity before taking further action.

In a recent article in *US Air* magazine, C.W. Metcalf reported that 75% of all sick days in the North American workplace are due to stress-related illnesses. The prevailing view in many organizations—"Let's tighten up, put our nose to the grindstone, and beat the SOBs"—may be responsible for much of that stress. That's because in order to bear down, you have to get stiff, and when you get stiff, you increase the chances of breakdown.

Is working harder, working more, really the answer? Cutting edge research in learning shows us that to be effective, a high tide of action must be followed by a low tide of reflection. Thus, the increased demand to get results is actually getting in the way of our ability to learn to be effective.

In these times of increased uncertainty and challenge, we need a good system of coordinates that allows us to find our bearings. Rather than pulling ourselves between the externally defined polarities of either-or, fight or flight, succeed or fail, we each must learn to find our bearings from an internal center of gravity that is inherently aligned with our values and natural desire to learn and move forward. From this inner state, we

"The people who have made the most contributions to the world have followed the cycles of withdrawal and return."
ARNOLD TOYNBEE

can re-collect our natural fluidity of thought and freedom to respond creatively to problems, no matter the external circumstances. When we learn to think in this way, our orientation changes from one of struggling rigidly to manipulate limitations and "get-it-all-done" to maneuvering creatively in a flexible dance of possibilities.

Thus, this chapter is an invitation to step out of the bureaucracy of your own mind for a few moments and begin to learn to find balance in the current reality. It offers you a solo practice to enable you to experience your body and embody your experience, a partnered practice to give you more options of response, and a small group practice field in which pressure is actually used to assist you in moving toward your own goal in any setting.

CENTERING HOME: FINDING THE POINT OF BALANCE

"You can only go half way into the darkest forest, then you are coming out the side."
CHINESE PROVERB

How you approach a moment determines where it will lead you. In the face of pressure, do you respond with distress or effectiveness? Do you see everything as a curse or a challenge? You can learn to master your personal energy in a way that goes beyond stress management. Like a sailor, you can actually use the winds of change as a source of energy. What is required first is knowing how to find your own center of balance—the pivot around which the compass needle of your life moves. This center is the point from which action unfolds and toward which it returns.

Thus, the first basic principle of finding balance in the unknown, as well as during the chaos of internal or external conflict, is centering, a process by which you integrate the habitually fragmented aspects of yourself—body, mind, spirit, heart, power, and common sense—back into their natural state of integrity. Practically, this results in an increased awareness of the moment and your presence in it. Rather than becoming a victim to whom things are happening, you become an active agent in your life.

Centering is reconnecting with yourself by increasing your awareness of what is going on, and accepting things as they are in your current reality. It is an opportunity to rest in the center of things. It is taking a pause to stop action, if only for a moment, or three breaths long, or for a morning, as if you were conducting an environmental-impact report on your own internal and external activity.

Centering is an invitation to pay attention in a different way, through the body as a living playing field, as an object of concentration, until you come to a still point, a place where your concept of yourself begins to open. From this place it is possible to turn inward in reflection or outward into action in a unified way.

The process itself is quite simple if you bring your curiosity and your willingness to be reflective and open to the unexpected. Each time you center, you invite yourself to release any need to be right, to judge, to anticipate, or to assume for just a few minutes. You come home to yourself by bringing your awareness into your body, acknowledging the truth of your sensations and emotions, as well as where you are in space and in relationship to other people around you.

Centering facilitates our capacity for being present in situations and emotions that otherwise overwhelm us, because the body becomes capable of containing chaos. By focusing on the bodily sensations produced by those emotions, it becomes easier to remain present with them and aware of their deeper nature.

"The physical center of the body is the part of us that remembers we belong to the universe."
GEORGE LEONARD

"It is better to conquer yourself than to win a thousand other battles, then the victory is truly yours, it cannot be taken away from you, not by angels or demons, not by heaven or hell . . . "
THE DHAMAPADA

Every time you connect with yourself in this way, you are stretching your inherent capacity to balance with the stress of continual change and challenge. Your perspective expands as your attention shifts from a rigid one-way-of-doing-things state of mind to an expansive strategic intuition that gives you a wider sense of the options that are available to you.

The solo centering practice that follows uses the awareness of your breath to bring you down closer to the trunk and roots of yourself by sensing your internal process. If you are upset, your breath will reflect that immediately, by becoming shallow and quick. Like water settling in a bowl held in still hands, if you keep your breath in your awareness it will calm by itself. You don't need to smooth the water and you don't need to try and make your breath settle.

PRACTICE ONE: SOLO
Centering in a Chair

⑥ Begin by sitting in a straight-back chair, with your feet flat on the floor and your knees opened to your preferred width. Experiment first by sitting vigilant in the chair as if it cannot be trusted to hold you and might collapse at any minute. After a few moments, consider how you would respond if you were startled suddenly from behind.

⑥ Now experiment by sagging into the chair as if it is a place where you can totally let your mind go on a little vacation. Totally collapse into the chair and, after a few

"I say to my breath once again little breath come from in front of me go away behind me row me quietly now as far as you can, for I am an abyss that I am trying to cross."
W. S. MERWIN

moments, consider how you would respond if you were startled from behind.

⑥ Next, explore developing a relationship not only with the chair and any anticipated surprising moments, but also with your breath and body:

Come forward in your chair. Notice the sensations in your body as you feel what it's like for your spine not to be supported by the chair back.

Notice your weight or heaviness on the seat. For 8-10 breaths, let the full weight of your torso sink down through your sitting bones into the chair. From within, allow your breath to give shape to your posture in space.

Notice how your right foot contacts the ground and the amount of weight it communicates into the earth. As you begin to inhale, start to develop more of a push with your right foot; as it pushes slightly, the rest of you remains relaxed and loose—as if on vacation. As your right foot pushes into the ground, wait for the sensation of the counter-push of the earth to stream into your body. Then release your foot and notice how that influences the rest of your body.

Shift the pressure to your left foot as you inhale. With each breath, allow yourself to let go of holding tightly in any particular way.

Alternate back and forth from right foot pushing to left foot pushing. Each time the pushing leg puts you into a new space, allow the rest of yourself to stay newly positioned and relaxed. Allow your belly to stay soft and expanded. Notice how your body can respond much as a sea plant does by swaying in a warm ocean current.

Pause, relax, and sense how you are sitting now. Take a soft breath, push both feet into the earth, and wait as your vertical alignment feels the effect of that push. As

"Perceive all conflicts as patterns of energy seeking a harmonious balance in a whole."
DHYANI YWHOO, Etowah Cherokee

you breathe, experiment with redistributing the support of your body weight between your feet and spine. Find the balance place where the mere intention to ground your feet produces an uplifting feeling throughout your body.

Now find a neutral position neither forward or back, in which you can sit without collapse nor exaggerated effort. Each time you feel your spine getting tired, bring your awareness back to your feet and breath and soften your body so it can tune into the new uprightness being negotiated in this space.

Imagine that your posture is not static but always adjusting to the earth—responding to inner currents or breezes. The more your feet push on the earth, the more it gives you a lift. Once again, consider how you would respond if you were startled from behind.

INTEGRATING THESE LEARNINGS INTO THE WORKPLACE

1. What situations in your life do you respond to by mistrustingly, vigilantly preparing yourself for the bottom to fall out?

2. What situations in your life do you respond to by letting yourself collapse?

3. What situations in your life do you respond to with curiosity and flexibility as in the third way of sitting?

4. Use your new practice to center while sitting during high-stress meetings, at your desk during a charged phone call, or in any situation where your habit is to lose yourself by focusing only on the task or the other people.

5. Itemize your own personal resources for centering. (For example, one attorney knows that he is centered when at the golf tee, ready to hit the ball. One consultant knows she is centered when

in her herb garden. A dentist knows he is centered when trout fishing.) Then, when you are in the middle of a stressful work situation, bring to mind your own personal resource. For example, the consultant under fire imagines she is in her herb garden plucking some pesky weeds; the dentist while preparing to do oral surgery, imagines, for a moment, he is knee-deep in a rushing stream reeling in on a fish.

THE UNDISTURBABLE MIND: CALMNESS IN ACTION

Stress has less to do with external pressures than it has to do with our overreaction to them with excessive tension (as in being rigid in the chair) or by our shrinking from them with an attitude of slackness (as in being slack in the chair). Most people think of the former as being strong or forceful and the latter as being weak. In fact, neither of these fight or flight reactions are maximally effective. If you are rigid, it is virtually impossible to move swiftly, impossible to shift directions with agility, a valuable asset for the fast-paced business world. In a similar way, if your attitude is to get to the top by stepping on others, you will always be on guard for who will be coming after you. Living a life adrenalized for perceived crisis provides a heightened sense of being alive, but eventually leads to collapse.

Many people in this day and age find it quite difficult to relax, even though almost everyone will tell you they think being relaxed is a desirable state. Many spend their lives alternating between attitudes of excessive tension and excessive limpness, both indicating a disconnection or fragmentation of body and mind.

When your mind is upset and is disconnected from an awareness of your body, your body tends to tighten, your energy

When we come to a point of rest in our own being, we encounter a world where all things are at rest, and then a tree becomes a mystery, a cloud becomes a revelation, and each person we meet a cosmos whose riches we can only glimpse."
DAG HAMMORSKJOLD

contracts, and chances are you will feel disconnected from people and circumstances around you because you're too rigid to adapt and move with them. On the other hand, if you are too limp, you compromise too readily, give in to the demands of others, lose initiative for life, and generally "don't care." This is frequently referred to as lazy.

The phrase "calmly energized" describes the centered state in action. When you are calmly energized, you feel comfortable in your body; your body feels light without sagging; you feel both gravity pulling you toward the center of the earth *and* the sensation of buoyancy from the centrifugal force of the earth. The image is of a top, spinning in equilibrium on its axis at maximum speed, rather than toppling over when it stops. True vitality has this calmness at its center.

When you are calmly focused on a task, your breathing becomes so subtle that it is almost inaudible. When samurai fought with swords, observers could often predict who would win the match by watching the breathing of the contestants. If one fought in fear or anger, his breathing reflected that state, indicating his mind was not calm and clear.

Centering helps you be flexible and adapt to changing circumstances at work. You feel comfortable enough inside yourself to allow other people to be themselves, and to choose to expand in the face of pressure, instead of allowing it to make you rigid and resistant.

Centering your body and mind means having a power that is relaxed and flexible, as well as non-confrontational. This comes from the realization that a fighting mind is doomed to fail and that tension diminishes your power. The more tense you are, the more your possibilities are limited. When you are open and aware in body, mind, posture, and attitude, you have the flex-

"Laziness, in my opinion, is not inaction, but rather inattention."
WENDY PALMER, SENSEI

ibility to respond and the courage to face change. You meet the challenges with curiosity, as if you were dancing with them, rather than fighting them or fleeing from them.

PRACTICE TWO: DYAD
Centering with a Challenge

Benchmark: Take a moment to consider your predominant stance or posture at work. What metaphors would apply? For example, are you, "steeled for trouble," "hunkered down for action," "halfway out the door," "never at rest," a "hand on the wheel" type? What adjectives would apply? Harmonious, controlling, light-hearted, angry, combative, hopeless, bitter, sarcastic, delightful, righteous? Take a few notes about your responses to refer to later.

"It is not that I don't get off center; I just correct so fast that no one can see me."
Morihei Ueshiba, O Sensei

This practice is done with a partner. As in the photos below, Person A will stand with his/her left leg one-half step forward. Person B will challenge that stance by pushing firmly with the fingertips of his/her right hand against A's left shoulder for a distance of one to two inches.

This challenge will be repeated three times and A will have the opportunity to use three different attitudes and postures in response to the challenges from B—aggressive, passive, and centered. The first two states of thought or response will probably be very familiar and might not require much practice; the third state may be non-habitual and therefore is accompanied by some practice suggestions.

Challenge 1

Aggressive: Person A should attempt to anticipate the challenge and to react by using strength to resist being moved.

What are the physical sensations of this way of receiving an energetic challenge? How would you characterize the relationship between A and B? Think of a time at work where this is the energetic dynamics between you and another person.

Challenge 2

Passive: Person A should attempt to anticipate the challenge and to be as pliant and accommodating as possible to avoid conflict.

What are the physical sensations of this way of receiving an energetic challenge? How would you characterize the relationship between A and B? Think of a time at work where this is the energetic dynamic between you and another person.

Challenge 3

Centered: A will bring attention to his/herself and unify body and mind: Release all stress from your body. One way is to rise up on the balls of your feet and shake your hands and wrists up and down at the level of your hips as if you were trying to shake water off your fingertips. Then slowly let this motion grow smaller and as you approach stillness, lower your feet until your heels just barely contact the ground, with your knees remaining flexible.

Lightly place your hand just below your navel and breathe into your belly, which is the physical center of gravity of your body, and focus your mind there. You might imagine the whole universe condensing into that place or a spring bubbling up and out from there, through your legs, trunk, arms, and head, and opening outward. As you allow the flow of energy, you can also expand your periphery so that your eyes, ears, and skin simultaneously sense, not only your own energetic presence, but also the presence of the world around you.

B now challenges A again, using the same pressure as before. Notice the differences in feeling and response.

What are the physical sensations of this way of receiving an energetic challenge? How would you characterize the relationship between A and B? Think of a time at work where this is the energetic dynamic you've encountered between you and another person.

Switch positions so that A is the challenger and B the learner.

Benchmark Revisited: Take a moment to refer back to the metaphors and adjectives that you began with. What did you learn from this practice that can give you more freedom in how you respond to events on the job? What can you do that allows you to practice making choices in how you respond?

INTEGRATING THESE LEARNINGS INTO THE WORKPLACE

1. Begin to respond to the challenge with a rigid, aggressive stance and notice what you need to do in order to return to a centered stance, such as widening your periphery or relaxing.

2. Begin in a collapsed, passive stance and notice what you need to practice in order to return to a centered stance, like feeling a current of life-energy flowing through your legs and hands.

3. Begin in a centered stance and notice what variables distract you toward aggressiveness or passivity: a look someone gives you? a picture in your mind? a story you tell yourself about a feeling you have? a tone of voice?

4. Ask yourself what this practice can teach you about stressful challenges.

5. Think of three situations in the workplace when you are living out each one of these three ways of responding.

6. Consider some of your colleagues who, when challenged, are habitually aggressively rigid or collapse passively. What have you learned here that might create a different effect?

RESPONSE-ABILITY

It's not what happens to us that determines who we are but how we allow it to affect us. We all have what we call "sizzle points," moments when, if we continue what we are doing, we'll boil over or implode. When we go beyond them, in effect, we have lost our choice of response. However, when we learn to notice our sizzle points as we approach them, we have room and time to maneuver and make choices, instead of having them made for us. Centering is a discipline that helps us do that.

"I've never been afraid to fail."
MICHAEL JORDAN

We can lose our ability to respond to ourselves as well as others. An indication of this is the fragmentation of who we consider ourselves to be: "Today is Saturday, so I'm a lover; Sunday, so I'm a parent; Monday, so I'm a manager;" or what we imagine we aspire to: "A part of me wants to go here, but a part of me wants to go there, and another part thinks that none of it matters anyway;" or in how we satisfy our basic needs: "I need to rest, but I have to finish this job and I really need to pay attention to my employees, but then I need some time to plan for next week and I need some exercise and fresh air." Then there is the fragmenting of emotions: "I'm terrified of all this downsizing, but I'm not going to pay attention to that because I'd be ashamed if anyone thought I couldn't handle this challenge, but I'm really angry that I should care so much about what other people think, and sad that I really can't find meaning in what I'm doing anymore." This is five minutes in the life of the average American mind! It's stressful reading about it, and crazy-making trying to live with it!

USING WHAT YOU CAN'T CHANGE TO HELP YOU CENTER

Centering in the midst of all of this chaos means remembering that you are more than the struggle. Rather than contracting away from it, or trying desperately to ignore it, you can learn to expand to include it, as if you are the sky and each of those fragments is a cloud blowing by. You notice each, name it, feel its effect in your body, acknowledge its presence, and hold it in the vast wide horizon of all of who you are. Yes, the fear is there. You are not ignoring it. Rather, it's as if you respond to it by bowing. Responding does not mean fixing, changing, or being overtaken by. It just means making space for all of that to exist, noticing it, and balancing it with all of the rest of who you are.

Centering in external chaos involves using "paradoxical thinking," which makes no sense to your linear mind. Most of us use paradoxical thinking to get uncentered; i.e., "the more John goes on and on that way, the more uptight I get." When you think like this, you are instructing your brain to run the software program for "upset" every time he goes on and on. But what if you put John's "going on and on" to work for you? What if, for example, you told yourself, "The more John goes on and on, the more I'll remember to center and notice my own breath." Or, "the faster he talks, the slower I'll feel inside." This way of thinking might not sound logical to your linear mind, but it is an effective way to use what you cannot control to help you connect to your own center of balance, instead of being used by it.

When you are centering in this way, you do not necessarily take in more information, but you do process it more effectively. It can alert you to what you need to know, give you insights into useful possibilities, and help you get a much clearer sense of the current reality, commonly known as presence of mind, or composure. It also helps you be less susceptible to irritating behavior in other people.

Here's an opportunity to use the power of your mind to transfer the principles you've been learning to a situation where you're being challenged verbally or psychologically. This can be a first step in providing your brain with another "software" package of responses so that habitual "knee-jerk" responses can be revealed and then avoided.

PRACTICE THREE: GROUP
Centering with Specific Challenges

Whether a stressful challenge comes in the form of a physical push, an auditory demand, or as a visual overload, energy is still being directed at you, and you are free to choose how you respond and what meaning you will choose to attach to the challenge.

Begin by thinking of the work situation where you are most likely to "lose it." ("It" means yourself, your center.) Take the essential ingredients of the situation that are most challenging to you and re-create them in the present as a role-play or simulation. For example, a loud, chaotic situation where someone is demanding a quick answer from you; being presented with volumes of visual data; being asked to deliver a summary speech.

Choose different people from the group to represent the different variables of your particular situation—perhaps

*"In the midst
of winter,
I finally
discovered
that there
is in me an
invincible
spring."*
ALBERT CAMUS

*someone can role play a demanding manager, someone else,
a passive colleague, and so on. In addition to these representatives of stress, you may want to create some representatives or coaches of centering. For example, someone could
be in the chaos next to you and lightly challenge you with
their hand to help you remember some of the skills from
practice 2. Or have someone sit in a chair next to you and
ask quietly if you feel your feet making contact with the
earth as you breathe (as in practice 1). Or someone could
hold up a visual cue to remind you that you are free to
breathe or walk.*

Centering home to your own body and breath is the essential
first step, no matter what's going on with the people around
you. Your habitual impulse may be to focus immediately on
what *others* are doing—to try to fix them, teach them, change
them, or prove something to them. Paradoxically, if you make
them the center of your attention, you lose your own balance.
Do you want to be right or effective? If, instead, you take the
moment to center yourself, you reconnect with your own power
to choose.

Be in charge of your learning by starting, pausing, stopping, and stepping out of the simulation if you need to in order
to think paradoxically: "The more they shout, the more I'll feel
the quiet in my center." This enables you to open to your own
resources without shutting anyone else out. You may even ask
someone to take your place in the simulation so that you can
observe compassionately and curiously from a distance.

*When you feel centered, open your curiosity out toward the
challenge with an attitude of open-hearted interest. Notice
what helps you do this—for example, walking around as
people talk, doodling, looking away, or humming to yourself*

inside your mind. The intent is not to accommodate or agree with others, but to find a more conscious and appropriate way of discovering where your leverage is in the situation.

INTEGRATING THESE LEARNINGS INTO THE WORKPLACE

1. After you practice, note in some way what worked for you. What helped you find calm during the "sizzle points"?

2. Ask yourself, What's the one thing I can do to apply what I've learned here to my workplace situation?

3. Is there a way you could elicit support from a "centering coach" at work, namely, ask someone to gently press on your shoulder, hand you a pad and pen, or ask you if you can feel your feet on the floor if he or she observes you "stressing out."

BUSINESS ANECDOTE

John, the CEO of a Midwestern company we consulted for, was a charismatic leader who thought of himself as collaborative and effective in fostering teams. We spent the better part of a morning doing these practices with the senior management staff. As we sat down to translate the relevancy of what we had been learning to the workplace, a wasp flew in the room and a woman screamed that she was allergic to wasps. Immediately, John grabbed a magazine, rolled it up, and stood on a chair to bat at the wasp.

Then Nancy, one of the administrative assistants called out, "Stop and center, everyone." Everyone immediately took three deep breaths, including John. Nancy walked over to the allergic woman, pressed on her shoulder as we had been doing all morning to remind her to come back in her body, and then

"Aikido integrates mind, body and spirit into harmonious relationship and inspired action. Because the art is physical it serves as an especially powerful learning metaphor for highly intellectual corporate environments."
CHRIS THORSEN

"To attain knowledge, add things every day. To attain wisdom, remove things every day."
LAO-TZU

said, "John! This is just what happens each time there is management team challenge. You take over, and we just stand by and let you." John smiled ruefully and rubbed his chin. "Instead," Nancy continued, "let's apply what we just learned here and now." John stepped down from the chair and handed Nancy the magazine. She put it down and asked the group, "What do you think the wasp's intention is?" One of the men shouted, "To get out. The windows are all closed and it's trapped." Someone immediately went to open a window, someone else got a glass and scooped the wasp into it with an index card. When he released it out the window, everyone cheered.

As we sat down to discuss what had happened, John said, "That *is* my pattern. It's what I always do. Very interesting. I kept doing it during the practices too, strong-arming and taking over. Suddenly, my old habits were very obvious to me. You all did much better without my interference." As he shared this, John got a standing ovation. In the months that followed, "remember the wasp" became a gentle reminder to center whenever any one started "taking over" or becoming passive.

GUIDELINES TO CENTERING

QUESTIONS THAT HELP:

"Do I want to be right or effective?"

"What's really important to me in this moment?"

THE PRACTICE:

- Release your body completely. Shake out.

- Notice your breathing three times, as you direct your attention to the center of your abdomen.

- Expand your periphery: See wide, listen wide, feel wide.

- Allow your weight to be "underside" and inhale "through the soles of your feet."

- Use paradoxical thinking: "The more X, the more I'll notice my center" or "The louder he shouts, the calmer I'll feel inside my body."

- For an instant, bring to mind a situation or place in which you naturally center, and use that to help you in the stressful situation.

3

How do we create trust and support on the job when everything keeps changing?

RELATIONAL LOGIC

Establishing Trust During Uncertain Times

"In the absence of certainty, one must have courage. Courage requires overcoming our fear of the unknown. . . . We are afraid of the letting go that chaos requires, because we believe our world will fall apart without strict control. And yet the new science of chaos theory tells us there is an underlying order to the universe that does not require our control, and that chaos can be a gateway to quantum leaps in improvement."

DANIEL KIM, *The Systems Thinker*

WHAT ARE YOU HOLDING ONTO ANYWAY?

heard from Jack Kornfield

In response to your request for additional information in block number three of your report form, I put "poor planning" as the cause of my accident. Here are the relevant details:

I'm a bricklayer by trade. On the day of the accident, I was working alone on the roof of a new three-story building. When I completed my work, I had five hundred pounds of bricks left over. Rather than carry them down by hand, I decided to lower them in a barrel using the pulley on the side of the building. Securing the rope at ground level, I went up to the roof, swung the barrel out, and loaded the bricks into it. Then I went back to the ground and untied the rope, holding it tightly to ensure the slow descent of the five hundred pounds of bricks.

You will note in block number eleven of the report form that I weigh one hundred thirty-five pounds. Due to my surprise at being jerked off the ground so suddenly, I forgot to let go of the rope. Needless to say I proceeded at a rather rapid rate up the side of the building. In the vicinity of the second floor, I met the barrel coming down. This explains the fractured collar bone.

Slowed only slightly, I continued my ascent, not stopping until the knuckles of my right hand were deep in the pulley. High up in the air, I had the presence of mind to be able to remember and hold on tightly to the rope. However, the barrel of bricks hit the ground and unfortunately the bottom fell out. Devoid of the weight of the bricks, the barrel now weighed approximately fifty pounds. I again refer you to my weight in block number 11. As you might imagine, I began a rapid descent down the side of the building. . . .

The tale on the preceding page points a mangled finger at an important principle: When you can't control what is happening, change how you are relating to it. We need to become aware of the places and ineffective processes where we are holding on obsessively and destructively. We need to disentangle from that which is unskillful and to release ourselves to learn in midst of the unknown.

ORIENTATION

The world of business today is swirling in the "permanent white water" of continuous change. Sometimes it feels like trying to turn a battleship around in a narrow, strong running river. No matter how effectively we use old strategies of analysis; working harder, being technologically and politically smarter, it is not sufficient to navigate these rapids. We've swum with the sharks, managed our minutes, controlled our quality and still the pressure to do more with less grows and grows. We are re-engineering our corporate structures, but we also need to re-engineer the minds that created those structures.

The core competitive edge seems to be an organization's capacity to operate in radical change at all levels. For this to occur, our thinking has to be the first thing to change. We no longer can hold on to our old rigid definitions, right answers, ways of doing things. It isn't chaos that causes us to struggle, it is our resistance to it. Because we cannot be certain, we have to be willing to learn, unlearn, and relearn individually and collectively.

A truly alive organization is always learning and developing. General Motors shifted from being in the business of selling cars to being in the business of maximizing its customers' mobility. Shell Oil shifted from selling gas to satisfying its customer's energy needs.

This metamorphosis needs to be conscious. Thriving depends on being able to assess the present situation accurately, communicate it effectively, be calm under pressure, and anticipate and react effectively to the currents of change. When information and decision making are spread among so many people, we each need to be able to think on our feet—lightly, autonomously, and ready at any moment to shift directions, as if we were in a rubber raft together. It is crucial to be able to pool and synthesize human resources in order to maximize effectiveness in uncertainty.

This chapter invites you to let go of the habitual ways you react to uncertainty. It offers you a solo practice to support your learning to trust yourself in the unknown, a partnered practice designed to help you learn to trust yourself with others, and a group practice for learning to trust the collaborative process.

"The seed that is to grow must lose itself as seed
And they that creep may graduate through chrysalis to wings.
Wilt thou then, O mortal, cling to husks which falsely seem to you the self?"
Wu Wei

RELATIONAL LOGIC: BEYOND COMMAND AND CONTROL

Perhaps we are so afraid of change because we have so little confidence in our ability to learn. Those people who have contributed the most to our society are those who are dedicated to lifelong learning and feel successful at it. If we trust this ability, then uncertainty becomes part of it all, the way a blank canvas is natural to an artist or quiet to a musician is the pause where the music is born. We can learn to use uncertainty more effectively. What if, for instance, we were less certain about how impossible things are? What if we stopped trying to control change and focused on changing what keeps us from expanding into our full capacity as human beings?

Drawing on new discoveries in chaos theory, Margaret Wheatley, author of *Leadership and the New Science,* described this approach in a keynote speech: "We need to consider how we can partner with chaos. To develop a strong core identity or center, an organization needs to develop the capacity to constantly self-update, stay connected, keep in touch, develop relationships, find necessary information, and know how to interpret that information. Much more of our focus needs to go into how we work together and how available we are to each other."

We have mastered the rugged individualism and competitive logic that once were necessary for survival. Now, we are being forced to find each other and orient with an entirely different kind of logic. Finding our bearings in the unknown is different from being on top of things. It involves a willingness to let go of opinions, beliefs, and assumptions about how things are and can be, a readiness to look and listen and feel in new ways, and a tuning to the possibilities that may be emerging in the present. Living in uncertainty calls for our whole-minded, whole-bodied, wholehearted presence in the midst of action.

THE CHALLENGE TO CHANGE: TRUSTING YOURSELF IN THE UNKNOWN

Change is a natural state. We ourselves are masterpieces of change. From instant to instant, cells are dying and being re-born. Like the river that seems to be the "same old river" when we step into it, the water that rushes around our feet is, in actuality, always changing, always new. Control is the illusion—trying to make something stay the same as it's always been, solid and predictable.

"Until you are willing to be confused about what you already know, what you know will never become wider, bigger or deeper."
MILTON ERICKSON, M.D.

Scientists have discovered that there is an order within chaos, even if it is not predictable. Thus, although we have to let go of the idea of constancy, we can still create well-ordered organizations. Relating to the uncertainty within ourselves is the starting point for finding balance within organizational instability. What is required is letting go of the old, rigid ways of thinking so we can learn to trust ourselves in the unknown. What is required is a willingness to walk through the chaos, sit in the confusion, and master the fear.

Take a moment now, and consider the changes that are going on in your life. How are you responding to them? What is it time to let go of? Most people deal with the fear and confusion that results from uncertainty by trying to control it. One senior level manager of a huge communications firm described his habitual approach as "paralysis by analysis." He hated disorder or confusion of any kind, so he commonly got more and more controlling, trying to "stay on track." The more he'd try to control the situation, the more rigid he would become, struggling until he found himself stuck in tunnel vision. All he could do was more of what he already had done.

In Aikido there is an adage that says, "When you meet rock, become water. When you meet water, become rock." In this case, when all that is around you is shifting and unstable (water), becoming rock does not mean getting harder and harder, as the manager did. Rather, it suggests becoming more comfortable with the flow of uncertainty, and rather than trying to manipulate what is external to you and impossible to control, come back to yourself, where you are free to choose to maneuver fluidly.

When most people encounter fear and/or confusion, their habit is to close down their thinking until they can find one

"Science cannot solve the ultimate mystery of Nature. And it is because, in the last analysis, we ourselves are part of the mystery we are trying to solve."
MAX PLANCK

right answer or the single best thing to do. We have learned to be so uncomfortable with the confusion of many possibilities that we try and kill off as many of them as quickly as we can.

But habits are not who we are. In our true nature, humans are remarkably flexible and adept. What is another way of relating to fear and confusion besides control, fight, or flight? When asked if he was ever afraid, Morehei Ueshiba, the founder of Aikido and one of the greatest martial artists in Japan, replied, "I feel what you feel, but you name it fear. I name it a call to action." Rather than trying to get rid of his fear when facing the uncertainty of a battle, the samurai would bow in respect of his fear, acknowledging its vitality. He would extend his awareness to the source of the fear, which is the experience of the energy in his body, rather than paying attention to stories in his mind about why he should or shouldn't feel it.

From this position, the brain can go from confusion to an ever-widening state of mind that is like a kaleidoscope where new patterns are constantly being created. In this expanded state of mind, your perspective shifts to the big picture; you think about the forest rather than the trees, you hear the music rather than the individual notes.

We have the capacity to be with things as they really are, and then, when we've found our balance with them, we can imagine what is the most wise and effective response. As a means to increasing your trust of yourself in the unknown, the practices that follow give you the opportunity to choose new responses to external and internal conditions of instability.

"Am I willing to give up what I have in order to be what I am not yet? Am I willing to let my ideas of myself, of humanity be changed?"
M. C. RICHARDS

PRACTICE FOUR: SOLO
Expanding Your Awareness While Walking

In order to learn how we can come to trust and support ourselves when relating to changes, we will spend ten minutes slowly exploring a process we take for granted—walking.

Pick a physical location in the space you are occupying, and walk directly to that goal. As you walk toward it, name to yourself what you are experiencing as you move. For example: "I am thinking about the best way to get to that goal and feeling pent-up energy in my chest."

Return to your original starting spot. This time introduce an element of change by walking toward the goal with your eyes closed. Name to yourself what you are experiencing as you move. When you get to the goal, pause and open your eyes.

For five minutes practice expanding your awareness by coordinating your breathing and steps: Each time you inhale, take a step on one foot. Each time you exhale, step with the other foot. Continue this slow one breath, one step walking for five minutes, keeping your attention present in this coordinated process.

Finally, randomly toss a dozen tennis balls or other objects into the space, close your eyes, and walk from one side of the space to the other. (Or if you have access to a child's messy room, walk across the floor of it in the dark!)

INTEGRATION QUESTIONS

1. What was required for you to operate as you encountered the changing conditions of darkness and random obstacles? For example: "It was necessary to think less of attaining the goal and more about how I was walking."

2. What did you learn about trusting your ability to navigate through the blind, random walk? For example: "I learned to trust my own rhythm even when it was very slow."

3. How did this practice cause you to rely on senses that you normally ignore? For example: "I had to rely on feeling my motion, the floor, and the objects instead of navigating with my eyes."

4. In what situations at work are you moving toward goals and operating in the dark on paths over uneven ground? What advice does this practice offer for dealing with change in that work situation? How could you use senses and abilities that are normally ignored at work?

5. What would be the effect of noticing your breath as you "walk" through each step of a meeting or project?

FROM DEPENDENCY TO INTERDEPENDENCY: TRUSTING YOURSELF WITH OTHERS

"Many of our culture's brightest individuals go into business. Some are able to see the pain inflicted by the business world and they are ripe for opening to the new opportunities that will arise from redefining business so that it serves the greater needs of both the human and non-human worlds."
MATTHEW FOX

The contracts we have built our businesses upon were created to establish security. But security is like a lamp on a night table. You depend on it to illuminate the darkness—until there is a power failure. Security is based on something external being the source of your stability. It gives the illusion of permanent stability. Safety, however, is the reverse—the source is inside of you and something on the outside becomes the focus—as if you had a flashlight in your belly.

We've tried to build secure structures, to resist change as we fear what might happen if we loosen our grip or let members of our organizations speak truthfully to one another. We're afraid things might fall apart, which is just what they seem to be doing. As we face the new millennium, the old social contracts that we depended upon for our security are no more.

They were based on certain implicit values, a spoken or unspoken "deal" that traded loyalty for job security. In *Fortune* magazine, Daniel Yankovitch, a marketing and opinion researcher, put it like this: "Companies are unaware of the dreadful impact they are having. They don't realize they are violating an unwritten but important social contract they have with workers."

No air conditioning filter in the world can screen out the resentment, anxiety, fear, and sullen compliance that permeates the atmosphere in many organizations, at a time when what is most needed is freshness, flexibility, and innovation. Maintaining commitment without the old carrot of lifetime security is becoming extraordinarily difficult. How do we create a safety that cannot be lost? What new deal would, in fact, increase our intellectual capital and facilitate our ability to navigate in the permanent whitewater of uncertainty?

What seems to be a loss or an ending may, if one steps back far enough to perceive the whole pattern, actually be a gain, a new beginning. Nobel prize-winning physicist Ilya Prigogine noted that living systems will fall apart when faced with radical amounts of change, but after that, they have the possibility to reconfigure themselves such that they work better in their environment. The radical change in perspective we are experiencing shifts us from the mechanistic notion of separate and discrete parts and pieces to one of interrelated wholes. Rather than thinking of ourselves and each other as "human doings," static instruments of production who merely focus on contracts and projects, we need to concentrate on partnerships and relationships that sustain and nurture us as constantly developing, learning, and renewing human beings.

Implicitly, workers are asking management to tell them about the new social order. Various companies such as AT&T, Chevron,

"New organs of perception come into being as a result of necessity. Therefore, O man, increase your necessity so that you may increase your perception."
Rumi

Albert Einstein was asked, "What is the most important question human beings can ask themselves?" He replied, "Is the universe safe?"

Prudential, and Intel are realizing that paternalism and codependency are dead and must be replaced with a new deal that is based on adult-to-adult communication and candor. Instead of the "father knows best" way, the new deal insists that employees think for themselves. Instead of being told what to do, employees are now expected to take initiative. In this model, communication shifts from a family style to a community approach. Job guarantees are replaced with incentives to enhance employability and develop diverse and competitive skills. Security no longer comes through loyalty but through one's ability to learn and adapt to new situations. Philip Carroll, CEO of Shell Oil, put it this way: "We have to insure that individuals are on a learning program that gives them the wherewithal to succeed, even if they can't stay in the company."

Have you ever leaned on a railing at the edge of a precipice? The railing provides a sense of balance and safety that enables us to stand much closer to the edge than if there were no railing. Yet this is a deceptive sense of security, because if the railing were to collapse, we would most likely collapse with it. The question then becomes how can you enjoy the support of the railing without trusting all of your balance to it. The same is true about work. We want to put all our trust in the security of the company, but fear its collapse. The following practice can help you deepen your thinking about the distinction between the dependency of the "old deal" and the possible relationships that can exist when uncertainty is made explicit.

PRACTICE FIVE: PAIR

Trust Bridge

Benchmark: As a reference point, think of a work situation in which there existed some issue of trust, loyalty, betrayal, and so on and take a moment to write down some of the people and particulars involved.

Option 1

Total Dependent Trust Approach:
Typically, people begin relating energetically to each other, a team, or their company in the following manner:

Person B forms an arched bridge by kneeling on hands and knees. Person A then bends over, and with elbows and forearms, leans on B. (Note: If the positions indicated are not physically comfortable, you may elect to practice this standing with one person leaning on another's shoulder.)

Person A commits full weight and balance to B trusting that B will remain stable. Both A and B take note of what it is like to be in this dependent relationship, trusting one to hold up the other and be stable.

Suddenly and without notice B collapses. Both A and B notice the results of this first way of relating.

Typically the verbal response would be: "I thought I could trust this person, (team, company) but I guess I can't."

Option 2

Distrustful Independent Approach

After people have been let down by enough situations like this last one, they often adopt the following strategy to avoid dependence by getting tough and rigid:

Person B forms an arched bridge as before. Person A then bends over and makes contact with elbows and forearms and goes through the motions of leaning on B, but doesn't trust any body weight to B. Both A and B take note of what it feels like to be relating in this fashion.

Suddenly and without notice B collapses. Both A and B notice the results of this second way of relating, which can leave us isolated and fragmented, disconnected from each other and unable to collaborate or care for others. A typical verbal response might be: "Look out for #1. It's everyone for themselves."

Option 3

Trusting Self With Other, Interdependent Approach:
Somewhere in between the first two options lives the "middle third."

Person B forms an arched bridge as before. Person A then leans over and contacts B with elbows and forearms, simultaneously maintaining a connection with B and balance with herself. Typically, this means that A will practice centering; (see practice two), breathe, calmly energize, widen periphery, and so on.

Suddenly and without notice B collapses. Both A and B notice the results of this third way of relating.

A typical response could be: "Who knows how long this will last? Let's do the best with what we've got. How can we connect with each other when one of us falls or makes a mistake? What can we create that we'll remember forever. Let's enjoy our connection while it lasts."

INTEGRATION QUESTIONS

1. Think of one situation at work where you allow your balance to be fully dependent on someone else. One sentence that would express that way of relating might be: "This is one team that I know will never let me down."

2. Think about a time when you had to hold something together, a time when you felt a whole project depended on you. Words that express that way of relating might be: "We can't live without you. We're counting on you. You are the only one who can help."

3. In what situations/relationships at work do you rigidly go through the motions of connection and yet never receive support when it's there for you? Words that might express that way of relating are: "Listen, anyone who's been around here for long knows even though they call us a team, you gotta look out for #1."

4. Think about a time when you were operating with a team that was only going through the motions. What phrases summarize what that experience might be: "Lights on, nobody's home;" "We weren't expecting anything;" "It's just a waste of time;" "We covered our asses and maximized personal gain."

5. In what situations or relationships at work do you manage to connect with others in an energized manner without losing your balance? A statement that might summarize that situation could be: "I've been through a lot of these downsizings, and all you can count on is what we can put together in this moment, and what life learnings we can have that can never be taken away no matter what."

6. What are the personal ingredients that enable you to relate to uncertainty in a way that simultaneously acknowledges connection and balance? Take a moment to write down what you learned from the practice that is part of your story for keeping your balance while you relate to others? How did you maintain connection without being totally dependent or totally separate? How did you avoid rehearsing or anticipating but still remain aware that change would come to the system that Persons A and B formed?

7. What did you learn as Person B about who you need as a support person or what you need when you let someone down?

8. What did you learn about trusting yourself to maintain a relationship through uncertainty?

9. As you go through a day at work examine each relationship in the context of this practice in order to understand the nature of the social contracts being played out. Examine how these play out in you personally. For example, in what cases do you respond like the dependent idealist hoping for a quick fix? In what instances do you respond like the rigid cynic expecting nothing? In what cases are you in balance with yourself and others? What

internal scripts, myths, or stories grow up around each type of response? Examples might be: "Every time I try to help, I get hurt." or "Every time I count on someone else, I get *let down.*"

Benchmark Revisited: What does this practice teach you about the situation you brought to mind in the beginning of this practice?

"Only connect."
E. M. FORRESTER

RENEWAL IN THE MIDST OF UNCERTAINTY: LEARNING TO TRUST THE COLLABORATIVE PROCESS

As we turn this corner in the evolution of business, we are being asked to shift toward structures that facilitate relationship, that link up people, units, tasks. We are being moved to partner each other in very different ways, ways that can move us out of old conflicts into comprehensive fields of interdependence.

Interdependent relationships within and among organizations are a key business asset and knowing how to nurture them is an essential leadership skill. In a recent study on collaborative advantage published in the *Harvard Business Review,* Rosabeth Moss Kanter observed thirty-seven companies and their partners from eleven parts of the world. She and her associates found that North American companies, more than others, "take a narrow, opportunistic view of relationships, frequently neglecting the political, cultural, organizational, and human aspects of partnership." She concluded that collaborative alliances require a dense web of interpersonal connections and internal infrastructures to enhance learning.

Active collaboration takes place when organizations develop mechanisms—structures, processes, and skills—to bridge differences between individuals and companies in strategic, operational, interpersonal, and cultural dimensions. A primary condition for this bridging is a willingness to move beyond what Chris Argyris of Harvard University calls "skilled incompetence," which is our tendency to act as if we know what we really need to learn most. We cannot do this until and unless each party is willing to let go—let go of the illusion that we are invulnerable, without needs, perfect creatures who learn without making mistakes. We need to let the other parties "inside," which entails a risk—the risk of failure.

In most organizations, the fear of failure remains the dominating motivational force of everyday life. In a fascinating study of the decision-making processes of major pension funds, for example, researchers discovered that investment decisions were not based primarily on ensuring the best possible return for the funds, but rather they were made in such a way as to minimize the "blameability" of individual investment managers. The unwillingness to acknowledge and learn from mistakes is the source of the greatest organization "learning disability."

Consider an example of the converse. Put a Post-it note on your telephone or computer with the following quote from Thomas Watson, founder of IBM, "If you want to succeed, double your mistake rate." The Post-it note itself provides inspiration, since it was born from the failure of 3M company researchers to produce a strong new bonding compound. Instead of firing those responsible, the management encouraged them to discover what could be learned from this apparent disaster. By snatching success from the jaws of failure, a new staple of office life was born and 3M made millions of dollars.

Similarly, the road to excellence in Aikido begins with learning how to fall without injury and how to yield without losing face. The messages are profound: If you become rigid to avoid falling, your stance will be weak; if you don't know how to be thrown, you'll never be able to properly execute a throw; learning from mistakes is part of practice; the teacher may have decades more expertise, but is respectful to the most inexperienced student. Everyone is learning together.

In your organization, what would have to happen so you could make a mistake without being considered a failure? What would have to happen so you could share the learnings that came from those mistakes? What would have to happen so you could express your frustration openly and receive support, without being made to feel foolish or put down? What would it take for you to stay present with coworkers after they had made a mistake, instead of abandoning them, attacking them, or trying to fix them?

Martial artists practice falling on a cushioning mat. We learn to cope with uncertainty best when we can practice making mistakes in a safe environment with support. The following practice will give you the opportunity to do just that, enabling you to discover and teach others what you specifically need for support.

"Many people dream of success. To me, success can only be achieved through repeated failure and introspection" SOHIRO HONDA, founder of Honda Motors

PRACTICE SIX: GROUP
Blindfolded Obstacle Course

Logistics

Create practice teams of 3–5 people. Mark out a rectangle (ideally at least 10 feet wide and 20 feet long) on the floor or ground. This can be done with chalk or rope or anything else that will delineate boundaries for your practice field. Make some blindfolds for one to three participants.

Choose and blindfold one or more participants to travel through the marked off practice field. The remaining participants will then create a maze by placing objects randomly in the practice area. These objects (at least ten of them) can include all kinds of items such as chairs, glasses of water, logs, bags of potato chips, tables, boxes, plants, attaché cases, and so on. In other words, whatever your environment offers.

Option 1

Dependent Relating: In this first practice attempt, the blindfolded traveler(s) is placed at one end of the learning rectangle, receives orders from the other group members, and begins to walk backwards through the maze. The traveler waits to be told exactly what to do and is totally dependent on the voices of the others to define location, progress, risk, and performance.

After the journey through the maze is complete, both the traveler and the outside team members/directors take a moment to notice the effects and the pros and cons of relating to each other in this dependent fashion.

Option 2

Independent Relating: In this second practice attempt, the objects are rearranged and the blindfolded traveler is placed at one end of the learning rectangle as before. This time the traveler chooses to walk backwards through the maze exactly as he or she pleases no matter what orders or advice are given.

After the journey is complete, both the traveler and outside team members take a moment to notice the effects and the pros and cons of relating to each other in this independent fashion.

Option 3

Interdependent Relating: In this third practice attempt, the objects are rearranged one more time and the blindfolded traveler is placed at one end of the learning rectangle as before. This time the traveler confers with the other team members and specifies the kind of support he or she wants or does not want from the group, what kind of risks he or she wants to experiment with, and what kind of debriefing he or she wants afterwards. For example, one traveler may want to develop the ability to feel his/her way through the maze without being told what's coming and may want coaching to take their time and experiment while enjoying the learning.

After the journey is complete, both the traveler and outside team members coaches take a moment to notice the effects and pros and cons of relating to each other in this interdependent fashion.

"A friend is one to whom one may pour out all the contents of one's heart, chaff and grain together, Knowing that the gentlest of hands will take and sift it, keep what is worth keeping, and with a breath of kindness, blow the rest away."

ARABIAN PROVERB

INTEGRATION QUESTIONS

1. Think of one project or function at work where you totally place yourself at the mercy of someone else's guidance. What are some of the tradeoffs of functioning that way? How would you characterize your learning in that situation?

2. Think of one project or function at work where you totally control another person's function and learning. What are the tradeoffs of that kind of relationship?

3. Are there situations at work where you go through the motions of being part of a team, get feedback, and then proceed as a loner?

4. Have there been times when you enjoyed handling a project or task with a group? What were some of the characteristics of the communication, division of labor, use of resources and competencies, debriefing of learnings and challenges, celebration, recognition, and so on?

5. What were some of the personal components of your preferred way of being coached through the maze? For example: "I want to have some experience in the maze and then ask questions if I need support." or "Tell me what I'm doing right instead of all the things I'm doing wrong."

"Surely all art is a result of having been in danger. Of having gone through an experience all the way to an end. All beautiful things that come out of us, come out of our faith in change, the mystery of life."
RUMI

BUSINESS ANECDOTE

At a strategy meeting of a large telecommunications firm, the leadership team was exploring how to maintain effective connections with internal service partners in unstable environments. The words "trust" and "distrust" kept coming up in conversations.

One participant said, "We are going to have to go back and present a plan about the future that will impact six thousand people's lives. Some of the people to whom we will presenting this idea will be expecting some new solution to their troubles. And, there will be the cynics who have seen so many ideas come and go that will try to blast anything out of the water.

"We really can't ask our employees to put their faith in their business unit any more, especially when we all know that the whole division is up for grabs in restructuring efforts. People are terribly wounded and angry, and they know they can't trust a company, a division, a team, or a leader to be there forever."

Then the meeting participants took time out from the conversations to practice the bridge (as in practice five). After, one woman said, "Initially I had a fear of depending on you at all, knowing the change that was coming; then I realized there is no reason I couldn't balance on you for a little while—I mean I wasn't falling over or anything. . . . I did not have all my weight on you but just enough to feel your presence and movements. And that way I could feel when the change in our system was about to occur and support myself." And one man who had been the bridge said, "I learned that I could fall or change without being abandoned and/or losing connections with the system."

When the practice was finished, the team concluded that the only thing they could guarantee in the midst of the chaos was the commitment to maintain relationships with each other. And given the uncertain nature of the future, this important unifying question became, What could they create together that, no matter what happened this time, would have value for all? One man went on to say, "This third kind of relationship is the kind I want to build with my internal customers in our company as well. Because if they're relating with me in either of the other two ways, they will either be totally angry and hurt when restructuring happen; or, if they are being totally rigid and cynical, they won't be flexible enough to relate through the changes ahead. This third way allows a flow in the system without discounting our efforts or giving up."

Many of us have experienced let downs and suffering when those we have leaned on disappear or fall down. And our response to that has been to attempt to live independent of one another in an autonomous, John Wayne "I don't need anybody for anything" way of relating. While autonomy is important and

"The organizations we work in (of the near future) will be far less stable in every way. The normal ways of defining ourselves—the normal structures that give us a feeling of solidity and predictability—will all have vanished."
MARGARET WHEATLEY

has its place, it is also limiting and illusory.

No success can really be an independent achievement. "Getting to the top" requires a rigid rush over people, producing the all-too-familiar loneliness at the top. This is also the state that many employees find themselves in after downsizing and reengineering. The basic lack of trust leaves us, as author and management guru Steven Covey puts it, "fearfully rushing to live, rushing to love, rushing to learn and rushing to leave a token legacy."

This rigid independence leaves us safe from others' collapse, but disconnected and cynical. We notice and care less and less about others' vulnerabilities; we are unable to trust people enough to work effectively in teams; we are unable to give or receive support.

Interdependence is a state of relationship where you are neither trusting the other, nor trusting only yourself. Rather you are trusting yourself *with* the other, be that a person or an organization. You are receiving the support when it is there, taking it in deeply into your own center, and when it collapses, you maintain your connection without collapsing yourself.

Shifting from the mechanical management of things to a people-oriented paradigm means we need to function interdependently, both autonomously and focused on creative, effective, synergistic interactions with people. Since we know there is no "forever" contract, we need to receive the support that is available in the present and use it to create the quality of life we aspire to.

GUIDELINES FOR NAVIGATING IN TIMES OF UNCERTAINTY

courtesy of
Judy Sorum Brown

- ◎ *Trust your own truth and speak about it;*

- ◎ *Value diversity, including the divergent voices within you;*

- ◎ *Express both professionalism and personalism;*

- ◎ *Presume collaboration;*

- ◎ *Notice the nature of your communication;*

- ◎ *Attend to your inner life;*

- ◎ *Consider change as vitality;*

- ◎ *Plan to learn from setback as well as advance;*

- ◎ *Keep creativity at the heart of your life;*

- ◎ *Be aware of your mental models, the lenses through which you are perceiving the world;*

- ◎ *Be courageous, remembering that losses may also be gains.*

4

BOUNDARIES, NOT BARRIERS

Respecting One Another's Limits

"There were always choices to make. Every day, every hour offered the opportunity to make a decision, a decision which determined whether you would or would not submit to those powers which threatened to rob you of your very self, your inner freedom, which determined whether or not you would become the plaything of circumstance."

VICTOR FRANKL, writing of life in the concentration camps

VALLEY OF THE BLIND

Based on "The Country of the Blind" by H.G. Wells

The hero of this story was an ordinary person, not much different than you or I. One day, motivated not out of a desire for the new, but out of fear of the old, he walked out of his life. With no particular destination, he found himself wandering in the desert.

After weeks of traveling in uncharted territory, he crossed a small mountain, and descended into a narrow green valley at sunset. There a small village was nestled. The pine houses were snug and inviting, with scarlet geraniums hanging from window boxes and wisps of smoke rising from brick chimneys.

The villagers welcomed the traveler enthusiastically, as if they hadn't had a visitor in a great many years. It didn't take long for him to realize, however, that everyone he encountered was blind. There were no lights anywhere, except for the glowing fires in the hearths, no street lamps, no neon signs, no road signs of any kind. Since everyone had been born blind, the whole village was designed to function in the cool of the night.

In the weeks after he arrived, the man was very impressed with the agility with which the villagers navigated through the streets by "reading" bumps with their feet that were placed strategically along the curbs. He felt great pity, however, for the handicapped townspeople. This kindled into a purpose—the traveler decided to stay to help them any way he could.

His passion was ignited when he met the mayor's daughter. In no time the man was completely smitten and wanted to live with her for the rest of his life. Plucking up his courage, he went to ask the mayor for her hand.

The reply he received was completely shocking. "My daughter, marry you? Oh my goodness, well, you seem to be a nice enough lad, but I couldn't allow my one and only daughter to marry a cripple! Excuse me, I mean someone who is so very handicapped."

"Me? Handicapped? But it is you all who are blind!"

"Blind? What's that? My dear man, you must understand that since you arrived here, we have had to take care of you. You are so disabled you cannot get from one place to another without tripping and falling or getting lost. You seem unable to function in a factory or at any job that could provide you with a wage. I'm sorry, but I just couldn't let my daughter marry into such a disadvantaged future as the one you offer her."

"But we love each other so much and . . ."

As the mayor turned away, his words sank into the traveler's mind. He realized that he was different from everyone else. Perhaps he was handicapped. After all he didn't function very well in the village. Maybe the mayor was right.

"Isn't there anything I could do?" he asked, "I can learn in time . . ."

The mayor tilted his grizzled head to one side and replied, "Well, it's the opinion of the town physician that those two orbs on your face make learning very difficult for you. They seem to create disturbances of some kind. The doctor thinks that if they were surgically removed, well, you might indeed be more like the rest of us and even be able to function here."

"Orbs? You mean eyes? You want me to have my eyes removed? Are you crazy?"

The mayor shrugged his shoulders. "Eyes? What are eyes? The decision is yours of course, but if you want to marry my daughter and live here, it is the only way."

The traveler was distraught. He couldn't imagine living without his new-found love, but the price seemed impossible. As the days passed, his mind whirled round and round on itself. Finally, he began to imagine what it would be like to become "normal" like everyone else. Not long after that, he agreed to the operation.

As he lay down upon the cold metal operating table, he was determined to cooperate. The surgeon, ready to begin, lifted his sharp knife and leaned over him. But in that moment, the young man's heart seized. Sitting bolt upright, he began to scream, "No! No! I will not be blinded just to be like the rest of you. No! My vision is a gift and I won't give it up. Absolutely not!"

The villagers shook their heads in pity as the man ran back the way he had come, never to return to the dark security of the Valley of the Blind.

As this story teaches, many groups, be they villages or organizations, provide policies that blind us. When our boundaries are challenged by a new situation, relationship, or job, we can experience our power or lack of it—to collapse under the strain, or to stand by finding the outer "no" that liberates the inner "yes" of our needs and values.

ORIENTATION

We inhabit a small but vital corner of history. There has never been a more exciting or challenging time to be alive. Approaching the turning of the millennium is so potent, rich in danger, and fertile with power and possibility. What we do now makes a profound difference. Yet one of the most common complaints heard in the business world is that people are moving through life with no experience of actually living it. Where once we walked, now we are running. Our lives are fragmented into hundreds of separate compartments, all seemingly predetermined. We operate as if we are supposed to be open to all external demands all the time. But our very bodies demonstrate the impossibility of this: Eyes, for example, are neither open

"People used to working with computers become impatient with the slower durations of everyday life. . . . Never before has time been organized at speeds beyond the realm of consciousness . . . . Events processed in the computer world will exist in a realm that we will never be able to experience."
JEREMY RIFKIN

nor closed all the time, but need to be able to do both.

In some very essential ways, the current attempt at transforming American business organizations—what is generally called reengineering—completely ignores the personal situations of today's employees. The pressures that are leading companies to rethink their work processes in order to be able to do more with less, improve productivity, contain costs, and improve quality are on everyone's mind. But what is out of our awareness and what organizations are blind to, is the role that family, community, and personal needs are playing in this process. The pressure these forces exert on workers' concentration, peace of mind, and capacities to contribute actually decrease the productivity and quality of work and affect cost containment through unplanned absences and lowered efficiency. There are many subtle and not-so-subtle ways the very heart of our lives is being attacked in our day-to-day activities, in the ways we relate to the people we love or work with. There are more coronaries on Monday mornings between 8 and 9 a.m. than any other time of the week. The average American working couple spends only twenty minutes a day sharing time together. The average father spends only thirteen minutes a day with his children. Families try to meld entirely different sets of imposed time into a liveable shared life, but each member often feels his or her inner sense of rhythm is being violated.

Once upon a time we had time to get into the rhythm of a task and find the delight of wonder as our minds wandered in and out and all around an idea. Now we are forced into "hypervigilence," a perpetual external focus without the restfulness and creativity of that musing. What we are left with is a back-to-back staccato rhythm of doing one thing after another. We experience a continual sense of interrupted thoughts that

"Fatigue makes cowards of all of us."
VINCE LOMBARDI

haven't been allowed to follow through to their natural conclusion. The "time-saving" flood of technology—speed dialing, pagers, laser printing, e-mail, fax machines, computers—simply makes it easier to cram more and more into our overfed left brains. The cellular phone and beeper mean that anyone can be contacted anywhere, at any time. Call-waiting means that any conversation can be interrupted at any time. Boundaries of time and distance have disappeared. Inner life is seen as something one has no time for, yet many of us yearn secretly for "time of my own."

U.S. Navy researchers have known for some time that the human system must have a rest period every ninety minutes. In a study of sonar screen operators, they discovered that their personnel would hallucinate and read blips that were not there or miss blips that were on the screen, if they were not allowed a rest cycle every ninety minutes. If we chronically deny ourselves these natural ultradian rest cycles, we run the risk of a broad range of stress related disorders and seriously impaired functioning.

"Life is so short. We must move very slowly." THAI PROVERB

The resistance to new ideas that managers feel from many workers, the excuses, and the failure to implement, very often come from this overload, this lack of reflective or private time. The new work environment requires collaboration and interdependence, but how do you make yourself safe if you have to say yes to everyone and everything? The natural and known boundaries as to where and when and with whom we work are gone now. Work stretches around the clock and lasts seven days a week. All we are taught in management seminars is how to say "yes" more enthusiastically.

Since the boundaries that kept us safe have dissolved, we have built barriers to defend ourselves, walls to define where the world of work ends and the rest of our lives begin. We resist covertly, we sabotage unintentionally in an unconscious attempt to carve out time and space for ourselves. Once the subtle cues of our bodies are ignored, we break down in sickness and accidents. Once the visions of our spirit are ignored, we become cynical and withhold personal resources. Once the caring of our hearts is rebuffed, we refuse to bond with others. Once the rhythm of our minds is violated, our thinking becomes rigid and brittle.

A door is neither open nor closed, but capable of both functions. When we learn to establish boundaries, to say no to what we need to close to without fear of losing our jobs, then we will naturally open and say yes. Each of us wants to be productive—it is in our very nature. And each of us needs some time to close to the external world and open to our thoughts, feelings, musings, and dreams. If we ignore these needs for reflection, we begin to wall ourselves off from our own deepest wisdom. We divide ourselves up and dole ourselves out in fragmented pieces, as if we were commodities to be traded.

To allow yourself to be deeply touched by the pain of what educator/writer Parker Palmer calls "the divided life" is to become illuminated by the insight that your oppression is not simply the result of external forces, but also comes from your own collaboration with these forces. It is at this moment of awareness that you can refuse to cooperate in the further diminishment of spirit and vitality. You no longer make something else the problem and you no longer *are* the problem. You now begin to establish a relationship *with* the problem. There is no punishment worse than conspiring in a denial of one's own integrity; and there is no greater reward than living in a way that honors it.

" We are in trouble now because we are in-between stories. The old story sustained us for a long time—it shaped our emotional attitudes, it provided us with life's purpose . . . We awoke in the morning and knew who we were. We could answer the questions of our children. Everything was taken care of because the story was there. Now the old story is not functioning— and we have not yet learned the new one."
BILL MOYER quoting THOMAS BERRY

This chapter is a learning field for disentangling from that which is unskillful and for nourishing that which returns us to our ability to act with integrity so we can participate wholeheartedly in our work. The solo practice for self-mastery offers a way to listen to the internal cellular no's being spoken to us all the time. The partnered practice for developing mastery with others offers a positive process for expressing negatives. The group experience for expanding our mastery of change increases our capacity to distinguish and collaborate with a wide diversity of personal needs.

ORGANIZATIONAL BARRIERS TO LEARNING

A recent research project by Lotte Bailyn, the T. Wilson Professor of Management at the MIT Sloan School Of Management, explored the question, "What is it about organizations that makes life so difficult for committed employees with outside involvements, such as families? What are the barriers to learning?"

One of the groups she worked with in a Fortune 500 multinational organization consisted of engineers who were developing a new product on a tight schedule. They were part of the company's effort to reduce time to the market. The barriers she uncovered to commitment, effectiveness, and learning were:

- ☯ the presumption that personal needs would be kept to a minimum and work needs always have first priority;

- ☯ the presumption that putting in long hours was a sign of commitment, loyalty, competence, and high potential, as well as an indicator of productivity;

- ☯ the presumption that employee time belonged to the company;

"Instead [of staying in the present unknown], what frequently occurs is that we try to take back control of the situation and shift our attention into the future."
WENDY PALMER, SENSEI

❻ the managers' assumptions that interruptions were necessary interactions.

The engineers complained, "If there's a problem, the way we fix it is to throw more time at it. We can't really work between 9–5 because of the continuous interruptions, so we get our best work done after hours and on weekends. But the situation is only temporary, just until this crisis is over."

Dr. Bailyn reports that the situation was not temporary, but the common belief that it was prevented everyone from a serious reconsideration of their way of working. Because people had to deal with their "personal needs" on their own, their only choice was to deal with them on an ad hoc basis which actually increased the degree of absence and tardiness that was of such significant concern.

Upon recognizing this, the company shifted control from the managers to the work groups and began to experiment with letting groups jointly decide on policies, as long as they met their stated work goals. This alone created the self-managed teams that had been the stated goal at this site for years. The engineers set aside particular times to work exclusively on their individual tasks, and other times for interactions, and thus kept the number of interruptions to a minimum. Following this policy, the group achieved an on-time launch for the first time in the history of their department.

One manager who was involved commented, "To seriously consider the personal concerns of all employees as fully legitimate requires redesigning many of the habitual ways of working: the way we schedule, allocate, and evaluate work, as well as the way we define what we consider to be valuable work in the first place."

This redesign is like creating doors where there had previously been walls. People build barriers when there are no structures that support the establishment of boundaries. It is the parent-to-child, "do-what-I-tell-you-or-else," methods of relating that are responsible for these defensive obstacles to learning. Shifting to adult-to-adult communication creates structures where people can establish the safe space they need in order to participate fully as equal partners in learning.

PERSONAL MASTERY: SERVICE OR SERVITUDE

It is no small thing to make a direct contribution to your own aliveness. Having a customer-driven orientation, for all of its tremendous contribution to American business, has been misunderstood and used as an excuse to transgress our own and each other's boundaries. There is so much pressure to say yes in the corporate world that we ignore the no's of our corporal world. In the urge to belong, we can become "entrained"—a gradual process by which we adapt to and adopt the prevailing rhythms around us—rather than follow our true needs.

Awareness does not begin with change. Change begins with awareness. We have to be aware of the sensations of discomfort or joy in our bodies to even know that change is needed. How many of us go through our day with pain in our neck, after sitting in one boring meeting after another? It's so easy to ignore the signal or assume it's due to sleeping in a weird way or playing too much tennis the day before? Without that awareness, we can go on in situations that are abusive or counterproductive.

Collaboration requires that we work closely with others, but the closer you come to others, the more important it is to know your own boundaries, needs, and vulnerabilities. When you create the time and space in your life to do this internal inquiry, you reclaim your right to choose, create change, and respect yourself in the bargain.

Your kinesthetic awareness can play a significant role in how you schedule your life. There is a difference between time awareness and time management. We can, for example, live mentally, relying on technology to record and plan and beep us into action. Body time, however, is a function of the complex chemical and hormonal processes within our own bodies. Without an awareness of body time, you grow out of touch, and become impatient in your relationships and with your emotions.

How do you experience time in your life? Is it an uphill run? Does it flow in fits and starts or move evenly ahead with little change of speed? Stephen Covey, author of *First Things First*, asks you to ask yourself, "What's one thing I could do that would significantly improve the quality of the time I spend at work?"

In the moment-to-moment ways that you choose to stay loyal to the whole system of your being—body, mind, and spirit—you expand the borders of what is possible. By increasing the space between the external demand and your chosen response—what some martial artists call the zero point—you facilitate your integrity. A moment where you notice not only the reaction of other people to what you do, but also the reaction of your whole organism.

To shift the ways we relate to time requires that we say clear and definite yes's to some uses of time and resounding no's to others. This can only happen when we reconnect with ourselves—mind, body, and heart. From this congruence, we can achieve power "to" rather than power "over."

Your body produces physical and biochemical responses to thoughts and activities. An example is the startle response that occurs when you step near the edge of a high precipice. Your body naturally signals its responses to any situation, actual or imagined. We have been trained as children to ignore or even attempt to control these responses—in school you go to the bathroom at recess, instead of when you feel the need. Some people view the awareness of physical sensations as self-indulgent and inconsiderate. As a consequence people have increased their ability to numb or disassociate from the signals of their body. This ability may be a great convenience for schedules, but becomes problematic when attempting to learn, to think in an embodied way, or to live a healthy life. Have you ever found yourself agreeing to some plan in a meeting and then later been totally confused or angry that you agreed? Somehow your body was signaling "no" to you on the spot, but you didn't notice.

The practice that follows is a way of reconsidering and reclaiming the data you have been ignoring or only felt safe enough to experience in private. It will give you the opportunity to increase your awareness of the inner language of boundaries that are being broadcast through your body. It asks you to set aside some "boundary time," without any apology or explanation to others or any need to achieve anything—except awareness.

"Life's problems are different for each of us, and each needs a different way of facing them. Therefore each of us has to create his or her own method. If you imitate you'll be wrong. You have to create it for yourself."
TAISEN DESIMARU

PRACTICE SEVEN: SOLO
Increasing Awareness of Body "No's"

"Almost anything is easier to get into than out of."
AGNES ALLEN

⑥ Begin by taking five minutes to notice what you are aware of in the present moment. Note the data that your senses experience for five minutes and speak or write that data down. For example: "I feel my feet resting on the floor; I feel my chest rising and falling with my breath; I see a beam of light on the floor; I hear the sound of laughter." Just take down the facts—unembellished sensual data, no comparisons, no analysis, and no stories. Do not, for example, embellish the sound with something like, "I hear the sarcastic laughter of some nasty creep." What is the effect of noticing five minutes of what is instead of what was or what you hope will be?

⑥ Now, think of an activity that you don't like. It may be something you do begrudgingly or with resentment. Next time, while you're in the midst of that activity, privately notice in detail and with curiosity your body's sensory responses to the activity; that is, what do you feel while approaching and participating in the activity? What sensation might be your body's way of signaling "no"?

⑥ Keep a written record that begins to catalog your signals of "no" or dislike, and again, just the sensual data, not the explanations why or stories or assessments. For example, you may notice a sinking feeling in the pit of your stomach. Resist attaching a story to that feeling or reaching for your Maalox to make it go away. Just notice it.

⑥ After you have begun to notice your sensations of "no," begin to go public. Bring your increasing awareness of body no's to a meeting at work. Jot down the signals that occur in that meeting. Don't ask yourself to express or act on the signals, just notice that they occur. For example, you may notice that your head begins to ache just as the one hour year-in-review speech gets underway.

"Energy follows attention."
WENDY PALMER, SENSEI

INTEGRATION QUESTIONS

1. Think vividly of a time when you stopped or paused or spoke your objections in a way that was effective. What were the elements involved? How did you create the conditions that allowed the best of yourself to come forth? Please notice what you told yourself about your fundamental needs and deep values that led up to the choices you made.

2. Think about a time when you overrode your discomfort or silenced yourself when you knew you did not want to join what was going on. What were the elements involved? What type of rationale or "left-hand column" did you use to justify your choice, such as what other people would think, what you expected of yourself?

3. What changes would you need to make in order to work in a way that defined and respected your personal boundaries?

4. If you were to say no to everything that leads to a loss of vitality, which current initiatives or projects would you be continuing?

5. What are the unspoken prices to you and others of pushing yourself beyond your personal limits?

MASTERY WITH OTHERS: THE CONSTRUCTIVE DECLINE

There are many situations when you can't change the other person or the outer circumstances. Nonetheless, you always have the choice to cease struggling and create personal safe space. In Aikido, this is called *ma-ai.* In the physical sense, this consists of the distance just beyond the reach of a punch or kick. It is also the distance which allows you to see the entirety of the person rather than just his or her face. It is a proximity that creates no anxiety or feeling of physical threat. Birds and other wild animals have an instinctive feeling for this distance, and will allow others to enter that space only after "checking them out." As humans in a Western culture, however, most of us have never been taught how to physically keep a sense of our own values and balance, while deeply receiving another point of view.

This distance gives you the time and perspective to cultivate and notice where there is room for skillful action, clarity, ease, and perhaps even compassion. It enables you to notice where you are free, instead of where you are stuck. Thus, you can change your relationship to the situation, as well as to the mental and physical state you are using to organize your power. The ramifications of this "change of mind" are unlimited.

When we are stuck and lose our mental flexibility, we create barriers to learning. Some typical indicators of those moments are when:

⑥ The relationship with someone or to a situation changes from collaborative to resistant;

⑥ You experience an emotional wound that won't heal;

⑥ You find yourself frequently preoccupied, reviewing the situation obsessively;

- You find yourself stubbornly refusing to change and building a case in your mind why you shouldn't have to;

- You experience difficulty in making a decision or getting your work done;

- You find yourself withdrawing and withholding;

- You try to maximize winning and minimize losing.

Awareness of the above indicators can signal a need to make a boundary—there may be a no you are experiencing, but not giving yourself permission to express. Aikidoist Danaan Perry says that under every conflict is a desire to connect. The following practice is about learning to connect and, at the same time, maintain a safe space or haven, to meet and receive contact within your own comfort level. It's about creating a gate so that you don't have to put up a fort or passively collapse, learning how to honor the need for connection and still be in charge of how that connection occurs.

"Aikido is not to fight with or defeat the enemy. It is the way to reconcile the world and make humans one family."
MORIHEI
UESHIBA,
O'SENSEI

PRACTICE EIGHT: PAIR
Maintaining Personal Space

Benchmark: Write down particulars that define the number of times in the last week you have given others a clear limit, a boundary, a condition, or a no. Also, take a moment to characterize the energetic dynamics between you and the other person. Some examples: good will, collaborative spirit, grudging compliance, outright conflict.

Practice

In this practice your personal space is represented by your partner's encircled arms. The arms define a space into which entry is by invitation-only. Metaphorically, the arms are like the perimeter of a garden fence which forms the line of demarcation to keep weeds, rabbits, deer, and dogs out. Pests permitted on the outside, but not on the inside.

Person B forms a circle by raising arms and joining hands, palms outward, and folding the fingers of one hand over the small finger and palm of the other hand. Person A, the challenger, simply pushes lightly against the circle, for a distance of one to two inches.

In this position, Person B can practice receiving a challenge from outside in three different ways:

Option 1

Aggressive or Rigid: One habitual way that you may respond is by trying harder and rigidly pushing back against the challenge. With this response preserving your space becomes a battle and contest of strength.

Notice the effects of this way of trying to protect your personal space. What happens if the person pushing against the circle abruptly stops the challenge and disappears? Where is the center of balance of the person trying to maintain their space?

A typical verbal scenario of this kind of energetic response to a challenge might be, "Who do you think you are, trying to barge in and tell me what to do? You're are out of line and it will cost you."

Option 2

Passive: Another habitual way of responding to a challenge to your personal space may be to give in or collapse.

Notice the effects of this way of protecting your personal space. How do each of you feel about one another? A typical verbal scenario might be, "Have it your way; I guess your project is more important than what I had scheduled."

Option 3

Centered: The best way to perceive and maintain personal space is to practice centering. If the mind is calm and alert, it can comprehend the precise moment when that space is crowded and act without hesitation to preserve the safe distance.

Person B begins by standing centered, arms at the side, practicing the principles described in chapter 2. Now create the circular space keeping your arms and shoulders relaxed and energized.

Person B may notice the temptation or habit to use force to preserve the circular space and can continue to center instead. Some metaphors that may help are to hold your arms as if they:

- ⑥ *were a perch for a very rare bird, and you want to keep that perch steady;*

- ⑥ *contained an infant taking a nap;*

- ⑥ *were a hose with energy flowing through it in a circular motion, and the energy of the challenge puts additional energy into the hose and increases the clarity of the perimeter.*

To avoid habitual responses like rigidity or collapse, you can use your mind paradoxically, as you did in the centering practice, by linking the challenge with a desired outcome. For example, you could say to yourself, "The more I'm challenged, the more I enjoy breathing."

Of course not all challenges are as polite or gentle as the ones you have been encountering. What if the stress increases and A pushes harder? When meeting such a strong oncoming challenge, you can use that circle to protect your space and, just before the point of strain, turn and roll like a revolving door, letting the energy go by.

As you are turned by the energy of the challenge, notice how your whole being turns so that you face the challenger, eyes open and with the circle of your arms still intact. You can be influenced by that energy, yet still maintain a boundary that forms an inviolate private space.

A typical verbal scenario might be, "I respect the urgency and importance of your demands and I'm not ready to respond to them at this time. I'll be ready in one hour." The Chinese indicate "no," by nodding, bowing, and stepping back. Thus they indicate they have received the other's need, respect it as valid, and do not wish to fill it.

Here's a Western way of doing the same thing:

☺ *Think about something you really want. Now imagine asking someone to give it to you and all they say is "no." And no matter what you do, that's all they say. Notice what you feel in your body.*

☺ *Now reverse roles. Imagine someone asks you for something he or she really wants, but all you will say is, "no." Again, notice how you feel in your body.*

This time do exactly the same as you did in both of the above cases, but imagine they or you say, "I respect your needs, and I'm saying no." Each time notice the effect in your body. Compare it to the first two times.

Benchmark Revisited: After you have practiced the above for a while, recollect the instances in a work week where you stated a clear limit or boundary to a coworker. Notice the number of instances and also the energetic quality in both yourself and others that accompanied that interchange. Compare them to the benchmark preceding this practice.

1. What are some of the stresses at work that you are internalizing or trying to strong-arm away? How could you respond to them with this bounded circular dance?

2. What do you need to do during your work day to meet and respond to them at arm's length, simultaneously protecting the calm and safety in the circle of your arms?

3. Think of a moment when you came close to "losing it" at work. If your body were a room to contain the energy you label as anger, what would it be like? Would there be solid walls, bars, darkness, windows, or blinds? Would it be cramped and small or expansive and open? How would you describe the room in which you felt safe enough to learn from the anger and at the same time be in charge of how it is expressed?

4. Find a metaphor for the space inside your arms that conveys ease, safety, and peace. For example: "Like a secure harbor;" "Like a well-weeded, fenced garden;" "Like arms around a sleeping infant;" and so on.

"Let the person who doesn't know how to be alone beware of being in community. Let the person who doesn't know how to be in community beware of being alone."
DEITRICH BONHEIMER

"Safety is the final danger."
RUMI

THE DANGER OF THE UNDIFFERENTIATED WE

With the growing emergence of team efforts, one common misconception is that we all must have similar needs, values, and vulnerabilities. People act as if being part of the team means merging into an undifferentiated "we." Again, a lot of resistance comes up because people don't want to lose their sense of identity. What if teamwork meant maintaining "I" with "thee" instead of getting lost in "we"?

Collaboration and learning occur only in settings that are open, deeply respectful of individual needs, and bounded. When people have not set limits or have agreed to more than their soul will support, the passion that localizes, prioritizes, or drives activity is missing and the collaboration will ultimately not succeed.

The motivation of "I should" is very different than "I want." Compliance produces a very different result than motivations that stem from an intrinsic plan that supports your values. Until people see that making clear boundaries and choices is an option and a necessity, they will exhibit breakdown or incongruent behavior. Thus, questions like, "How far is enough?" become critical compass points by which to steer. Such questions are essential if we are to care for ourselves without rigidly denying others' needs.

This next practice is about exploring how you can define and protect your individuality rather than having to defend or compromise it while working together; without that distinction, people withdraw their resources even if they seem to go along with the crowd.

PRACTICE NINE: GROUP
Coming to Standing

Begin practice with the smallest group possible, you and another person. Sit on the floor facing one another. Draw your knees up toward your chest, and make contact by joining the soles of your feet and firmly grasping hands. From this sitting position. The task is to pull yourselves up into a standing position without breaking foot and hand contact. Attempt this task with at least two different leadership styles:

Authoritative: *Have one person be in charge and tell the second passive partner just how to accomplish the task. For example: "Look at me. Put your feet against my feet. Link your hands like this . . . no . . . that's not right, etc."*

Then reverse the leadership position and attempt the task one more time. After you are finished, share your learnings of what it was like to be in each role.

Collaborative: *Attempt the task utilizing such collaborative skills as reflection, joint inquiry, awareness of your process, and individual needs and images. Give each other feedback as to how you are feeling. For example, "Let's figure out the most effective way to link our arms. . . . How will we know when it's time to begin, pause, or put the big push on?"*

After the task is complete, share your learnings. Review what worked and how mistakes were used to increase knowledge and shared vision.

Larger Group Practice

Increase your group size to four and attempt the same task in the same two leadership styles as above. As you practice, have someone else write down the ideas, learnings, and results from the group interactions.

Keep increasing the group size and notice the evolution of learnings as "limits to growth" problems appear.

INTEGRATION QUESTIONS

1. What is one thing you learned about the communication of boundaries, limits, and needs that could be applied to a work situation?

2. As the size of the group increased, what did you learn that could be applied to the issue of scale in your organization?

3. What did you learn about the balance between reflection and action, between personal need and stated goals?

4. How were "mistakes" related to?

5. How were individual team member's needs, fears, and ideas responded to?

6. Was there any celebration of incremental learning and success? How would or did that affect the desire to continue learning?

LEARNING AND COMMUNICATION THRESHOLDS

Diversity issues have typically focused around gender and race. Recent research also indicates that we have very different styles of thinking, communicating, and learning. Creating mutual respect also involves understanding that there are differences in thresholds—points where people overload or distract easily. This requires that we learn to communicate those needs, and come to appreciate others' different thresholds.

Characteristics Of Different Learning Thresholds

High Threshold:

This is where we can concentrate easily, organize easily, and do detailed thinking. This is where we seem to be the most logical and is the mode most easily remembered.

Visual: Makes lists; has direct and persistent eye contact; can work at visual tasks for long periods; and is a person for whom "showing" is customary.

Auditory: Speaks articulately, persistently, and directly; has extensive vocabulary and spends long periods in detailed conversation; and is a person for whom "discussing" is customary.

Kinesthetic: Is action and hands-on orientated; organizes in piles and works systematically; needs to move and jiggle; likes things concrete; and is a person for whom "doing" is customary.

Low Threshold:

This is where we are most easily distracted, where we seem to think in webs or circles. It's often more difficult to remember or find thought here. Since this is where overall or whole thinking occurs, details are more difficult to deal with. This is where we feel most shy or private.

Visual: Is "eye shy"; prefers a low amount of visual input; sees the big picture; may take a long time to find visual images, dislikes detailed visual diagrams or instructions, may get lost on reading or a visual image.

Auditory: Is easily overloaded on too many words; remembers tone of voice, but may easily forget names and lyrics; can hear the whole symphony and harmonics; asks evocative questions that are difficult to answer; needs silence to think and find words.

Kinesthetic: Is easily distracted by touch; may sit still and inactive for long periods of time and get lost in movement; may start one thing, and then shift to another, and then another in no apparent order.

INTEGRATION PRACTICE

Create a communications handbook that contains a page for each person. It can include what was learned in the collaborative effort under the heading of: "If you want to treat me well . . . " "One boundary I have to tell you all about . . . " In addition, each person can describe his or her high and low threshold. For example:

- ⑥ "I have a low auditory threshold. If you want to treat me well, don't give me too many verbal instructions."

- ⑥ "My boundary is 'don't fill in my words for me.' I need time myself to sort through what I want to say."

- ⑥ "I have a high threshold for doing things. Feel free to ask me to help you do something that is difficult for you."

This little handbook can prevent untold instances of grief and conflict. Before you go to your next meeting, glance through its pages at the people who will be attending and notice what each needs for support and clear communication. Why attempt to read each other's mind when it can be so simple to teach each other what we need?

BUSINESS ANECDOTE

In a firm consisting of fifty consultants and twenty administrative support staff, there were bitter complaints about disrespect, arrogance, and hierarchy. Staff turnover was rapidly increasing. In this company, everyone stated that one of their most important values was respect. But living out that word was not possible when the support staff and the consultants each meant something different. Both groups used the same word, respect, but they were speaking two completely different languages.

We began to find common ground by having them do the embodied practices in this chapter. After exploring the practice described in this chapter, a conversation revealed the need for some awareness of communications thresholds and boundaries.

What surfaced was a pattern of the consultants, most of whom had a high auditory threshold, of walking up to support staff, most of whom had a low auditory threshold, and interrupting their paperwork with loud, fast conversation that culminated in a list of verbal requests and demands. The support staff felt totally distracted and rudely interrupted. They, therefore, reacted defensively. One woman spoke for the group as a whole, saying of her boss, "I know he doesn't respect me because he crowds me, and tells me everything, including the tiniest details in a very loud voice, as if I'm too stupid to figure them out from a memo!" The consultants, on the other hand, were "put off" when seemingly simple requests from them were met with confusion and "bristling."

When it came time to create the communications handbook, the support staff, most of whom had a high visual threshold, defined a need to receive their workload by visual memos and e-mail. This provided the means to schedule conversations ahead of time, allowing them to define periods of uninterrupted work periods during the day. Conversely, the consultants defined their need to receive communications in conversations and voice mail and not to be flooded with visually complicated paper input and e-mail. Understanding these differences in preferred ways of receiving information made all the difference. When the consultants scheduled conversations, they then felt as if they were being received instead of rebuffed. One consultant summed it all up: "It had gotten so bad between Joanne and I that I was

"We do not believe in ourselves until someone reveals that deep inside us something is valuable, worth listening to, worthy of our trust, sacred to our touch. Once we believe in ourselves, we can risk curiosity, wonder, spontaneous delight, or any experience that reveals the human spirit."
E. E. CUMMINGS

trying to get her replaced. I thought she was hypersensitive, ineffective, and had something against men in general. She was writing these complicated, emotional memos and e-mails about our work together and behind my back she was calling me an SOB. The air has cleared since we've both considered that the friction was about communication styles instead of a personal vendetta. She's even starting to laugh at my jokes again."

The practices of personal space and boundary setting, combined with the concepts of communications thresholds provided a context for the previous friction that, until then, had been personalized to particular people. This new frame for understanding made it possible to learn and evolve instead of bristling and withdrawing in pain.

From these and many other similar events, we have found that these embodied practices become mirrors to help us see, more clearly, our habitual mental models, our stagnant assumptions, and our fragmenting ways of relating that freeze us into isolation and incompetence. They also serve as magnifying lenses to increase our awareness enough to make different choices in how we respond to one another.

5

*How do we find personal intent and shared vision
in the distraction of day-to-day work challenges?*

VIRTUOUS
INTENT

Acting
On

Your
Vision

---

*"To know what is important to you, to have a real sense of who you are
and what would be deeply satisfying and archetypally true, is not enough.
You must also have the courage to act. . . . Courage is a willingness to
act from the heart, to let your heart lead the way, not knowing what
will be required of you next, or if you can do it."*

JEAN SHINODA BOLEN

THE QUIET IN THE PLACE WHERE THE MUSIC IS BORN

It is said there is a tribe of artisans living on the east coast of Africa that is known all over the continent for its fine carvings, as well as the unusual way in which they craft them.

As the sun rises over the Indian Ocean, the people gather in small groups on the edge of a crescent-shaped, golden beach. They each cluster around a large chunk of dark native wood. As the waves slide in and out over the glistening sand that reflects the enflamed sky, the people get quite still and place their hands on the wood. They tilt their heads to one side then the other. It is said they are listening for the song that is captured in the wood.

One person picks up a carving tool, then another does the same. A third squats on her haunches and begins to rock back and forth slowly. It is said at this point that the song's whisper has been heard. The people begin to carve away everything that interferes with its release. Some sit and listen, supporting the work of the whole. Some gouge, others file as they eliminate whatever seems to cause static. Chips fly as all are guided by the growing clarity of the song.

It is said that these people do not think of themselves as carvers, but as liberators of the song that waits in the wood.

The music of our individual and collective futures can be heard through listening deeply to our hearts as well as our minds, our intuitive insights as well as our reason, our core wisdom as well as our mental models. This requires carving away our usual ways of coping—relentless activity, sensory overload, rationalizing— to foster the release of what is trying to emerge through us.

ORIENTATION

A recent study suggested that 80 percent of American workers are unhappy in their jobs. What is at the heart of this discontent? At a systems thinking conference, Meg Wheatley told an audience, "We see the darker side of human beings, because we put people in bad jobs that make them feel worthless."

At the approach of the new millennium, we are being called on to reinvent the world while we reinvent ourselves. Our challenges are not just of measurement, but of spirit and emotion. Life in this high-turbulence environment shows that much of what used to pass for good business practice is no longer working adequately. Keeping our heads above water is not enough. In the world of command and control, what passes for commitment is actually compliance—we sit at our desks, doing exactly what is called for, functioning from the neck up and dead from the neck down, refusing to relinquish the ultimate freedom of choosing when, how, and why we engage our hearts and spirit.

You can't command passion. In it's place, we may succumb to the carrot of extrinsic rewards, giving up hope for enriching or joyful work, and devoting ourselves to advancing our careers. But our hearts aren't in it. And that ultimately affects the bottom line. Working for the customer and for each other is taking the place of working for the boss. While jobs are disappearing, work is everywhere. So, instead of asking, "What jobs are available?"—we're beginning to ask, "What is meaningful work?" The question, "How do we do it?" now is becoming, "Why are we doing it?"

Having become grounded in the boundary-setting skills of no in the last chapter, we now have the space to explore finding yes, which is the individual and collective intent that fuels forward movement.

INTRINSIC MOTIVATION

Experience of the recent past tells us that if the purpose of a business or an individual life is only to make money, what results is mediocrity. Until now, the basic premise of all of our institutions has been that if we are not motivated by rewards, we would do nothing. We have been trained to seek external approval and extrinsic motivation from the time we entered school: We sat and waited for a teacher to tell us what to do, how much to do in a given period of time, and how well we've done with the little smiling or frowning faces on our papers. This old mental model was based on the assumption that humans don't naturally want to learn or be productive. People were trained into running as fast as possible after the carrot and away from the stick.

"The crime is that we're asking people to only contribute 10%."
MARGARET WHEATLEY

However, that just might not be the most effective way to motivate. In a survey done in 1977 of research on the effects of rewards, psychologist John Condry found that people who are offered rewards tend to choose easier tasks, are less effective in using available information to solve new problems, tend to be more answer-oriented, are illogical in problem-solving strategies, and work harder in activities of lower quality and creativity.

Many current management techniques emerge from the very belief system they are trying to change, and continue to feed the need for approval by focusing on external reward systems and appraisals. But what if the basic premise upon which we operated was that all humans are designed to learn joyfully? What if we assumed that we are intrinsically motivated, and function naturally with dignity and self-respect? It takes only a brief time with a baby learning to walk to realize the truth of this. No one has to motivate that baby. He or she is a masterful learner and has a natural intuition to move ahead. Rewards?

The simple joy of risking the reach. No carrots, no sticks—approval is nice, but not necessary. Innately, we are all masters at learning from experience, at making mistakes and discarding them, at redirecting ourselves toward what works and is effective. This is how we are designed. Unfortunately, our institutions are inconsistent with our nature.

Peter Senge defines one of the cornerstones of an organization that learns as "aspiration," which consists of both personal and shared vision. And because planning is based on a future that is predictable—and the one we face is not—we must seek a broad, transcendent vision.

We are all part of a quest for deeper personal and organizational meaning; we want to feel original in our will, connected in our purpose, and working together to build something that feels real. This chapter offers experiences that help transform work into nourishment for life. The solo practice for mastering oneself offers a way to recognize the inner indications of your own intent. The partnered practice for developing mastery with others is about using distractions and challenges to assist in the focusing of that intent. The group experience for expanding mastery of change focuses on increasing the capacity to develop and support shared vision.

DO YOU CREATE YOUR WORK
OR DOES YOUR WORK CREATE YOU?

What if change—fear of it, avoidance of it, struggle with it, resistance to it—were not the issue at all? What if *development* were a more accurate term for what is trying to emerge—the pattern of forward movement, evolution, intention, and the

"Everyone likes the idea of pay for performance, but most of us have rarely experienced it. We most often get paid on the basis of how our boss evaluates us. This is more accurately called, 'pay for compliance'."
PETER BLOCK

ongoing expression of potential? Development is a natural phenomenon. It shouldn't have to be driven, for consciousness always seeks expansion. We need only remove those constraints to movement that build up in ourselves and our organizations.

In *Teaching the Elephant To Dance*, author Jim Belasco maintains that an elephant can be shackled by a flimsy chain that it has the power to break. By chaining it while it is very young and too small to break free, it becomes trained to the limits of its confinement. Thus, in a sense, the elephant is shackled by its training, not the chain. Belasco sees organizations and individuals living the life of the trained elephant, and individual and shared vision as the key to teaching the elephant to dance outside of those trained boundaries.

Human intention is at the very core of intellectual capital. The fundamental substance of an organization is the directed energy of its people. Not only the mental and physical energy we have habitually harnessed in the workplace, but also the emotional and spiritual energy we have largely ignored. In the martial arts, personal mastery involves finding your vision or intent in order to unify all of this energy and distill it into directed action. The same must also be true of organizations. Thus, developing shared, wholehearted vision is essential to the expansion of intellectual capital and the development of a true learning organization.

"The soul would rather fail at its own life than succeed at someone else's. . . . Our only real job is to garden ourselves as fully as possible."
DAVID WHYTE

LIVE AS IF YOUR LIFE DEPENDED ON IT

Most motivational programs and infomercials depict successful people with high-end bank accounts driving high-speed, high-powered sports cars and yachts. Is that what people's deepest dreams are really about? Is that what is at the bottom of the core images that guide you? Is that what motivates you?

Here's an experiment to reveal the strategies you habitually use to motivate yourself:

Pick a day when you are at home. For the entire day, make the commitment not to move until you have noticed the impulse to do something three times. The first time, refuse to move. The second time, notice what the impulse is like. How are you motivating yourself? Is it a voice in your head? Pictures? Feelings in your body? What is your main motivational strategy? Do you use the carrot and stick? Rewards? What other possibility? The love of doing it? The third time, notice again and then move.

Many Native American tribes believe that purpose must circulate through what they call "the four-chambered heart." The first chamber represents being wholehearted about your intention. The second represents being strong rather than weak-hearted about what you want to create in the world. The third is moving only on what you feel clear-hearted about. And last is living in such a way that you are open-hearted and generous with the energy that runs through you. Finding your intention then is simply a matter of discovering what you feel strongly about, what you're willing to bring your whole heart to, what you feel clear about realizing, and what you care so deeply about that it splits you right open.

"Back in the old days," when things were simpler and the river seemed to run smooth and straight, navigation was merely a matter of asking yourself questions that had finite answers, such as, "Who do I want to be when I grow up?" "What's the target I'm aiming for?" We were taught to set goals and muscle our way toward them by sacrifice, strength of will, discipline, rewards, and punishment. We could clearly measure if we were getting closer to our destination. It may be that goal setting and measurement only sit at the surface level of meaning, a surface that is now turbulent and chaotic. What calls you, pulls on you, sings to emerge from the deepest levels?

Imagine a stick in a stream, perpendicular to the current. We stand on the shore, separate from it, measuring the stick's progress as it is being pushed downstream. We ask reasonable questions, such as how far do we want it to go in a day? Questions that have quantifiable answers. Now imagine that the river becomes turbulent, roiling. What happens to the stick's progress? How do you measure it? How do you set a course for it?

Consider this possibility—What if the stick were a bamboo reed, and you cut off the ends so its hollowness becomes openness? What if your hand, with clear intention, turned it parallel to the current of the river so it would be less likely to get stuck or create blockages? The reed would then have its own form and also be aligned with the energy of the river.

Aikidoist Terry Dobson named this type of alignment "virtuous intent." It is quite different from asking yourself how much money you want to make next year or what goals you'd like to set for yourself. Virtuous intent requires opening yourself up to the full identification of all of your energies—physical, mental, emotional, spiritual—by aligning yourself with a current of deep purpose and meaning by asking yourself opening questions such as, "What is life asking of me?" or "What dream is pulling you?" These questions are dynamic rather than static. They make it possible to feel a coherence within all aspects of yourself and

"Don't ask what is the meaning of life but what is life asking of me?" VICTOR FRANKL

the world—what Thomas Merton called "the hidden wholeness." When you navigate in this way, your life, in fact, becomes a structure, a conduit for channeling this ever-changing vibrant current.

Virtuous intent also requires that you open yourself up by noticing another current, what composer/consultant/author Robert Fritz calls "current reality." This includes both your inner and outer experience of reality. Some of us habitually block or filter internal awareness, others external awareness. For example, a senior executive in a major electronics firm described himself as a "left-brained sort of guy, a logical thinker who wasn't much on intuition or emotions." This story that he repeatedly told himself became his core image. This self-concept blocked any possibility of his noticing his inner reality, because his awareness of feelings or images or spiritual guidance had been rejected. His brain's internal software program said, "This does not fit with the identity I have chosen. Reject this awareness."

Finding his virtuous intent meant being willing to put that old story about who he was on the shelf, and face the unknown emptiness that came with the blank pages of the new book he was authoring about his life. This could only happen when he allowed himself to notice all the currents of energy in motion (emotion) that ran through him daily.

The practice that follows is designed to increase your awareness of the yes's that are alive in you. It is meant to begin "opening the reed," so your motivation can, indeed, be intrinsic in origin.

"It is no failure to fall short of realizing all that we might dream. The failure is to fall short of dreaming all that we might realize."
Dee Hock

PRACTICE TEN: SOLO
Finding Your Inner Intent

Part 1: Increasing Awareness of Body Yes Signals

Just as you did in the solo practice in chapter 4, begin this practice by taking five minutes to notice current reality. Stay just with what your senses are aware of in the present moment. Note the sensual data by writing it down or speaking it. For example, "I see sunlight striking the carpet; I hear the rustle of papers; I feel cool air on the back of my neck." Avoid embellishments, comparisons, or analyses such as, "The sunlight that is leaving fade marks on the cheap carpet and creating a temperature differential that is causing winds to rustle the papers and make my shoulders feel cool by comparison, a factor that was obviously not considered by the architects who designed this space."

After five minutes of practice, begin to think about some activity or experience that you enjoy and that makes you feel more alive. It may even be something you do rarely, but nevertheless love.

While thinking about that activity, notice with curiosity the details of your body's sensory responses. What are the ingredients that produce your body's way of saying yes to something that you love? Is it like a movie that you are pulled to step into? Is it a feeling of aliveness you remember? Is it a voice in you that urges you on?

Make a list of your signals of yes, just the sensations, not the reasons why you feel them or the stories about them. Some examples might be: Breathing that eases in your chest, warmth across the back of your shoulders; tingling in your feet and hands; the release of formerly tight muscles; a sense of opening in your chest as your shoulders drop.

After you have practiced noticing the sensations of yes, while alone, begin to do it in public. Bring your increasing

*awareness of body yes's to work—moments as ordinary as
conversation over coffee, a minute of alone time, or the
moment of relief when you see a good report. Please resist
the temptation to make meaning of the "yes" feelings; just
notice when they exist or don't exist at work.*

Part 2: From Tension to Intention

*Holding one of your arms straight, raise it to shoulder height
and then let it fall. Raise it half as far and let it fall twice as
easily as it follows gravity back down. Raise it half again as
far and let it fall with twice the ease as it naturally responds
to the pull of gravity.*

*Continue the process of halving the distance and
doubling the ease until you are responding to the buildup
and release of energy but hardly moving your arm at all.*

*Finally, several times without movement, simply feel the
energy impulse that is the intention to move and the release
that is your arm returning to a natural alive stillness.*

*As you breathe with your arm resting in that stillness,
be curious when you feel the next impulse to move growing
in your arm. When you feel it, allow your arm to follow at a
rhythm and to a height of your choice.*

*Allow it to remain there until you feel the natural pull
back toward the restful position of hanging at your side.
Follow that cycle of impulse to move-movement-impulse to
release-release-and so on, for five minutes.*

INTEGRATION QUESTIONS

1. How is following the impulse to move different than forcing your
   arm to raise against gravity? What are situations at work where
   you naturally follow impulse? What are situations at work where
   you struggle against it?

2. When you are engaged in a routine work activity, what can you notice about your impulse to act, your impulse to rest, and the cycles that connect them?

3. How is it different to trust that the impulse to move is natural instead of something you have to will, discipline, cajole, or force?

4. Think vividly of a time when you functioned productively with simple delight. What were the elements involved? How did you create the conditions that allowed the best of yourself to come forth?

5. What are your gifts, the things you enjoyably do well, your natural capabilities?

6. What story about life would you have to give up in order to consider the possibility that you could function with excellence without forcing yourself to be someone that you are not?

KITES CRASH IF YOU LET GO OF THE STRING

In dreams begin responsibility. This means first responding to what you feel most passionate about and then responding outward by finding a way to channel that energy into the world.

But how do you create the forward movement that's necessary to become what you believe? In Outward Bound challenge courses there is something called a "pamper pole." Basically, it is a 30 or 40 foot telephone pole complete with climbing spikes staggered up either side. Hanging some distance from the pole is a trapeze. The challenge is to climb up the pole, stand on the top, and then leap off to the trapeze.

A CEO of a western utility company tells of his experience with the pole: "I knew I was completely safe because I was in a harness with lines held taut by my teammates. Still, I was

"There is a vitality, a life force, an energy, a quickening that is translated through you into action and because there is only one of you in all time, this expression is unique. And if you block it, it will never exist through any other medium and be lost. The world will not have it."
MARTHA GRAHAM

terrified, and even more terrified to admit to them how I was feeling. I am supposed to be their fearless leader after all."

Shaking his head back and forth he said, "It was exactly the same situation as I face at work. I had a hell of a time climbing to the top of the pole and standing up, but once I did, I just wanted to stay there or climb back down. That's not really true. I did want to risk the leap over to that trapeze, but I'm not sure why. I was frozen on the top of the pole, stuck holding tight to the old structure. I heard my team members shouting encouragement. Suddenly, I remembered setting my parakeet free when I was eight years old. My parents were furious, but as I watched him fly away into the woods, I was truly happy for him. The next thing I knew, I let go of the pole and risked the reach to a new possibility."

This man's forward movement began with an image. That's true for all of us, in one form or another. Stories, metaphors, and images are a deep way of knowing that speak directly to and through our bodies; they explain how things work, what to expect, and why things happen the way they do. For this man, his image of the liberated parakeet opened his mind to new perceptions and possibilities while the one of the fearless leader created a limited thought pattern that froze him on the spot.

Robert Fritz says that the important thing about a vision is not what it is, but what it does. As this example shows, guiding images serve as the strange attractors around which we build structures for action. Anthony Phillips, Director of Interesting Projects Inc. in Toronto put it this way: "Ten years ago everyone galvanized around images that pushed people to buying and doing things—the bulldozer effect. Now we're shifting. We want

"New guiding images / metaphors lead social development and provide direction for social change. They have, as it were, "magnetic pull" toward the future."
O. W. MARKLEY

to pull people towards things, we want to illuminate possibilities for action—the candle effect."

If we create images that foster fear, we can create quite a push. But moving away from what we are afraid of is not the same as moving toward what we really love. If we create myths that trigger conflict, we can create a different kind of push—the push against—the struggle to overcome opposition at all odds. But when the opposition is removed, we fall on our face. Pushing against what we oppose is not the same as moving toward what we passionately want to bring into the world.

So why don't we just create positive images to sponsor our passion? If we think of our intent as a kite flying in a high wind, why in the world do we ever let go of the string? Parker Palmer describes five fears that cause people to let go of the kite string: the fear of not being enough; the fear that the world is chaotic and coming apart; the fear that the world is basically cruel; the fear that one can only count on oneself; the fear that it isn't possible to survive loss. Each of these is based on a myth that would serve as a plot for Stephen King or a bedtime story for our worst enemies. Each will push you off balance enough to cause you to let go of the kite string.

If you turn each one of them over, however, and face up to the light, here are some alternative images that can help you move forward: Each of us has untouched capacities we only find when we challenge ourselves to risk; chaos is always the precursor to creation; nature teaches us that the world is incredibly generous and abundant; we are intimately connected to each other—one butterfly in Italy can cause a storm in Texas; every loss opens up to renewal in nature.

"Organizations enact metaphors. To manage an organization as if you were operating a mechanism, steering a ship or wielding a weapon, is to embody that metaphor in action. Managers may unwittingly construct a reality they dread through an incapacity to reflect upon the metaphor in use."
GARETH MORGAN

ENGAGING THE WIND

In Aikido, as you move forward from your center, you have to be willing to engage with whatever forces you meet. *Engagement* means a willingness to change course and be changed, without abandoning your virtuous intent; being willing to step into conversations that may seem at odds with your intent; being willing to come to these conversations with 100 percent of yourself, exploring the truth of the moment—yours and the people who are part of your current reality; and being willing to share your passion, your pain, and the vulnerability that comes with both.

Engagement means working with the internal and external energies you encounter, the way you would with the wind if you were flying a kite or sailing a boat. You don't try to control the wind, slow it down, or speed it up. You harness it and use it to take you where you want to go. Here's an example: A book publishing company found itself buffeted by a change in the prevailing winds of time away from books and toward multimedia. As they searched for their kite, they found their intention to make a difference by disseminating new knowledge in the world, no matter what form. Knowing that, they could prepare to use the wind by creating new structures in multimedia distribution.

When you are committed to your intent and hold a guiding image, your brain will act on your behalf as if it were on mechanical autopilot. Autopilot is an amazing homing device. A pilot for a major airline recently said that on his weekly flights from Boston to London, his plane was actually off-course over 90 percent of the time, but the autopilot continually corrected itself and the plane always reached its destination. An autopilot is the perfect metaphor for a guiding image for it is not each separate action that determines our effectiveness, but our actions over time.

As the next practice demonstrates, when we know our intent we can relate to the distracting forces we meet in such a way that they assist us in our forward motion. This is using what has been called the principle of "least action"—doing more with less by aligning with what is natural. Our ability to do this depends on whether we use core images and stories that limit our ability to engage those forces or expand it. Becoming aware of which images or stories you are using is the first step to choosing ones that are the most effective in maintaining your intent.

"Strength has more to do with intention than with the size of your biceps. It has more to do with your Spirit and your energy flow than the number of push-ups you can do."
TERRY DOBSON,
SENSEI

PRACTICE ELEVEN: PAIR
Moving Forward From the Chair

Benchmark: Think of a situation or person at work that is holding you down—where you find yourself spending a lot of time and energy butting heads instead of being enjoyably productive. Note it for future reference by describing the situation metaphorically. For example, "It's like a battle for turf . . . like pushing a rock uphill."

Logistics
You will need a straight-backed chair.

Person A begins by sitting in a chair while Person B leans on the sitter's shoulders with his or her forearms.

Person A attempts to get up from the chair and walk straight ahead, while B attempts to keep the sitter in the chair with an even, downward pressure.

Both people notice and discuss the dynamics of how they were relating. What would be some phrases or metaphors that characterize the dynamic?

Now try the practice again but this time A collapses in the chair under the pressure and both notice how that collapse affects the energetic dynamics of the relationship.

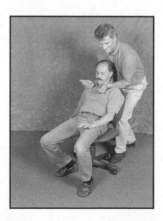

In the next attempt, A centers in the chair (refer to practice two in chapter 2) in order to be comfortably energized with the challenge. Then A vividly imagines a vision existing at a point across the room, something he/she really wants. Because this vision is deeply cared about, it produces an attraction or impulse to move toward it.

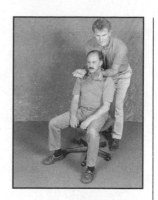

Even as A feels this impulse beckoning, simultaneously he/she can use the weight of the person above to amplify the direction of the magnetic pull. A metaphor that might help is to imagine being toothpaste in a tube with an open top pointing toward where you want to go. When the push comes from above, A can be propelled like toothpaste toward his/her intention. Thus, the downward pressure can be welcomed as added energy to propel the sitter toward the destination. In this way, A can allow himself/herself to be drawn forward, moving straight ahead without having to push up against the person above.

Benchmark Revisted: Again, bring to mind that situation or person at work. If you weren't butting heads or struggling, what would the intent be that you

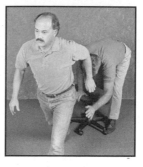

would be moving toward? If that person weren't engaged with you, what would he or she want to be moving toward? How would you describe metaphorically each of you moving toward what you want?

INTEGRATION QUESTIONS

1. Bring to mind a project where most of your energy is spent on pushing through difficulties, "fighting fires," rescuing, and so on. What is the vision that supposedly drives that project? Does that vision pull you and the other players forward? If not, what proactive intention would magnetize you?

2. What needs are met by reactive struggling that could be met in another way? For example, one man stated that pressure was the only form of connection and contact known to him in that moment. In the same pair, the sitter reported that he felt he had to push back to be manly. Once these dynamics surfaced, the players could redefine connection and manliness on their own terms.

3. Is there any vision in your life (work or otherwise) that pulls you toward it, instead of your having to work to get there?

"I have not a shadow of a doubt that any man or woman can achieve what I have, if he or she would make the same effort and cultivate the same hope and faith."
MAHATMA GANDHI

WITH A LITTLE HELP FROM MY FRIENDS

West Africans say that each of us must find our vision alone, but return to the tribe to realize it. Truth is not just in here or out there, but between us as well. Perhaps this explains the strong pull toward community and teams we are experiencing in the last decades of the twentieth century.

Physicist Neils Bohr declared, "The opposite of one profound truth is another profound truth. The opposite of an ordinary truth is a lie." The necessity of fostering the unique intent of any individual and the need for all to contribute to the collective wisdom of a group are both profound truths. If we are to move beyond the fragmentation that threatens to destroy our society, we need to create structures that hold both poles of these paradoxical truths in such a way that they can balance each other.

The CEO of a Midwestern consulting firm, when given the opportunity to devote a day to both personal intent and shared vision, insisted that dedicating time and energy to the former would undermine the latter. "What business is it of ours what people's private dreams are?" he insisted. "We're paying them to live our company mission. I don't want anything to distract them from that." On the other hand, the director of marketing for a large manufacturing firm expressed the opposite point of view. "Our guiding image is an eagle. Eagles don't flock. We want strong individuals here who even compete with each other to achieve the kind of excellence we expect."

Is it possible to actually create structures that support both personal and shared vision? Listen to the kinds of questions that a design team of senior executives responsible for "turning the bamboo around" after the trauma of downsizing came to one of our seminars and asked: What is the essential intent of each person in this room? What is his or her unique capacity to deliver that? How do we play to win—together? How can we serve each and thus serve all? What do I care enough about to choose to belong fully? What do I have to do so you can count on me to do everything I can to guarantee your success? What is the essence of this organization? What is our unique collective capacity to deliver that? What are the core questions, the

"If one is lucky, a solitary fantasy can totally transform one million realities."
MAYA ANGELOU

ones that if we knew the answers to, we would know what direction to move in?

From Quantum Physics we have discovered that we and our world are mostly space. Margaret Wheatley suggests that this is actually a field of consciousness, teeming with information and resources that we participate in whether we are aware of it or not. "If we have not bothered to create a field of vision that is coherent and sincere, people will encounter other fields— the ones we have created unintentionally or casually. Field creation is not just the task for senior managers. Every employee has energy to contribute; in a field-filled space, there are no unimportant players."

The word *consciousness* means to know together. In the African-American musical tradition, spirituals don't have a single authorship or ownership. The community makes the music; the music belongs to the community.

Pegasus Communications, Inc. (Cambridge, Massachusetts), a company that publishes materials and sponsors conferences on systems thinking and organizational learning, is a community attempting to make the music of consciousness. Every six months, the company creates a context and set of activities for an off-site retreat to revisit their shared vision and explore its implementation. Together they capture the current collective myths and images, look at work flow, and examine complementarity. Their guiding image is becoming more of a peninsula instead of the isolated island they were in the first few years of the company's history.

Performance reviews are "personal development reviews" where each employee meets with the president and another colleague to share their personal vision statement. These visions include specific intentions for one, three, and five years, as well as an assessment of current skills, and the development opportunities that exist. The company often has half-day off-site meetings where employees feedback to the larger group the results of their personal development reviews including what they are proud of and what they are struggling with.

They meet in supervision sessions once a week to identify their accomplishments, discuss what kind of support they need to move in the direction of their vision, and co-develop strategies. The group writes personal letters to each other describing how their contributions are meaningful to the whole. Their weekly meetings shift leadership from person to person, and focus from department to department so everyone has a sense of the whole operation. Bea Mah Holland, who serves as president, describes a significant change in the organization: "We've shifted from doing *to* each other to doing *for* each other to doing *with* each other." Daniel Kim, one of the cofounders, shares, "Our unique contribution toward building learning organizations may lie in our ability to know intimately the space we inhabit and how we contribute to the overall spirit of the enterprise."

If you were part of an organization like this, what would it bring you? How would it allow your own virtuous intention to flourish? What contribution would you make to its operation? The practice that follows can be an incubator for these questions.

"Each of us should be the change we want to see in the world." GANDHI

PRACTICE TWELVE: GROUP

Moving While Linked Together

Logistics: Form into groups of 6–10 people.

⑥ Each person privately picks a spot in the room. Imagine that this spot holds a fascination or pull much like the personal impulses noticed in the previous practice.

⑥ Join in a circle by interlinking arms; this linking symbolizes how personnel are joined by the organization's mission or vision. For example, people linked in order to build the ultimate recreational vehicle or people linked to provide the best information processing in the world

⑥ At a signal each person in the circle, at the same time and without words, tries to introduce the circle to their favorite spot by vigorously pulling the circle toward their pre-selected place.

⑥ After three minutes of this type of nonverbal advocating, each person stops, and in silence notices the effects of leading the group toward their spot in that way. What are some of the individual metaphors that describe your efforts? For example: "Like a tug of war struggle, pulling together and apart."

⑥ Unlink arms and pause for several minutes to digest what you have learned from your first attempt. Given the dynamics that occurred the first time, think for a moment how you might improve on your attempts to introduce the group to your favorite spot or point of view. For example, one team member reported that if she went with the overall direction of the group at first, she later noticed opportunities when she could more easily influence or steer the group her way. One man noticed that it helped to think of the circle as a living system, namely a caterpillar. His curiosity about helping the animal move as a unit eventually allowed him to bring the caterpillar to his goal, whereas in the first attempt, he had failed to bring the group to his goal.

⑥ Again, join arms and notice how, with the benefit of what you have learned, you can be more effective at introducing the group to your point of view.

INTEGRATION QUESTIONS

1. If your favorite spot represented an important personal dream, value, objective, or competency, what would it be?

2. What's one thing you learned in the practice about advocating for your intent in an organizational context?

3. Given that your employment in the organization is not a guaranteed or forever "done deal," what is one thing the company could support to take you one step closer to realizing your dream?

4. Given your organization's current business purpose, what is a valuable skill, resource, or competency that you contribute to the overall success?

5. What is trying to emerge in your group? That is, what unspoken awareness, concepts, or operating principles did your group agree and act upon the second time around? For example: The sum of the parts is only part of the whole.

"To be fully alive is to act: action must involve the discovery of reflection, the reformation of ourselves."
PARKER PALMER

BUSINESS ANECDOTE

Managers from the new products research division of a large utility were under heavy pressure to downsize. At a strategy-planning meeting, the one thing everyone agreed upon was how difficult it was to introduce any new plan because of the atmosphere on the job. This was summed up with such phrases as: "a powder keg ready to blow," people going off in a hundred different directions like the Fourth of July, obsessive data-gathering before action; apathy and complacency; passive-aggressive behavior; brutal backstabbing; and extreme cynicism around any new initiative.

The discussion following the "moving forward from the chair," practice eleven, revealed that the loyal senior employees were bitter, angry, and were pushing back against a pressure to change and automate. Some of them were being passed by in promotions in favor of younger hires with no company history but more training in automated systems.

After the "linked arm practice" (practice twelve), the discussion revealed that the senior employees were moving toward the goal of being loyal to the company as they knew it, whereas the new hires were trying to steer the group toward a high-tech data processing approach, which included major personnel cutbacks. The company's implicit long-standing policy to reward loyalty was being violated because of pressures to change quickly. These loyal senior employees felt deeply betrayed because their old goal of company loyalty and compliance was no longer valued, and they had no new vision in its place.

A new proposal emerged, in which employees were not offered lifetime security, but rather training of their choice to increase their employability no matter how long their job lasted. The senior employees were offered retraining and placement in other areas of the business, where compliance was highly valued.

ON CREATING A VIRTUOUS INTENT

(Things to think about while driving in traffic.)

- ⑥ What do you want to make possible for yourself today?

- ⑥ What really matters to you today?

- ⑥ What way of being would you love to nourish, cultivate, awaken in this day?

- ⑥ What do you care most about bringing into being today?

- ⑥ What do you feel prepared to give today?

May the intentions of your heart be beautiful.
May they bring beauty to all of the life around you.

6

THE MIDDLE THIRD

Transforming
Impasses
in
Thinking

*"Is it possible that we are completely alone and intrinsically connected
at the same time? If so, can we find the right tension between these two
extremes? Just as a string in a musical instrument is stretched to exactly
the right tension to create the proper harmonic sound, perhaps we can
learn to balance the tension between the paradoxes of life."*

WENDY PALMER

AND SO IT GOES

Perhaps it was Russia or Africa. Some say Tibet, some say Montana. This story is told in many countries. But always it involves a poor farmer and always it begins with a wild stallion charging up to his barn unexpectedly one morning. The horse, although dirty and uncared for, was a magnificent dark creature, with flowing mane and tail. When the farmer opened the gate to his pasture, it reared up on hind legs, pawed the air and then galloped into the field.

By sunset, the news of the stallion had spread through the village and the other townspeople gathered around the field to witness the horse charge up to the fence and then charge off in another direction.

An old man who lived down the road spoke to the farmer in an exuberant voice, "You lucky man! This morning you were the poorest among us, without even a cow for your milk and now you own this marvelous creature, worth a king's ransom. The other villagers nodded and shouted agreement, but the farmer merely shrugged and muttered, "Maybe yes, maybe no."

At sunrise the next day, the farmer sent his son into the field with a rope and instructions to break the beast for riding. When midafternoon came and still the young man had not returned, the farmer went out to investigate. The gate was wide open and the farmer's son was lying in the far corner, unconscious, with a broken leg.

Again at sunset, the villagers gathered, having heard the news from the doctor. The old man put a gnarled hand on the farmer's shoulder and shared sympathetically, "You poor man. Your only son unable to walk because of that ill-gotten creature. Now you have no one to help you work your fields. What awful luck!" The rest of the townspeople whispered their regrets, but the farmer once again shrugged and mumbled, "Maybe yes, maybe no."

"Western
culture has
taught us to
'think apart'
the world—to
divorce fact
from feeling,
spirit from
matter, self
from commu-
nity . . . But
these great
opposites co-
create reality.
When we think
them apart,
we destroy the
wholeness that
they can bring
to our lives."
PARKER
PALMER

A few weeks passed uneventfully. Then, one Sunday, a troop of uniformed soldiers galloped into the town square. A colonel, wearing a bright red jacket with gold epaulets and shiny, black boots, strode up the town hall steps. After nailing an announcement to the door, he shouted to all gathered that the country was at war and that every man over the age of eighteen and under the age of forty would have to join the army immediately. As the dust of the men being marched out of town settled, the old man turned to his neighbor, and said in amazement, "How lucky can you get! Your son is the only young man in the village not to have to go to war. If he hadn't broken his leg training that horse, he would be marching off with the rest of them to be killed. You are truly the luckiest man in this town!"

The farmer shuffled his feet in the dirt, and said quietly, "Maybe yes, maybe no."

The capacity to find the light in the dark and the dark in the light are at the essence of our ability to balance in what has been called, "the middle third," the fulcrum or turning point of any situation. From this place, it is possible to develop a creative relationship to the circumstances that exist in one's life.

ORIENTATION

If we are going to change life in our organizations, the first thing that must change has to be our rigid ways of thinking: reactivity, fragmentation, and overdependence on competition. It's just not the true picture for, as Peter Senge states, the walls or "chimneys" that separate different functions within an organization into "warring fiefdoms" are the results of fragmentary mental models.

A circle represents wholeness, it is said, for it is seamless, without division. But our habit is to cut it in half, lay it out in a line, and call one end true or right and the other false or wrong. We are so accustomed to this duality in thinking, this splitting reality into opposites, that we don't know how to deal with polarities when they are present simultaneously. We have become a nation of decision makers. Yet the word *decide* has the same root as *homicide, suicide,* and so on—it means to kill a part of. Thus when two polarities are present, we describe ourselves as confused, see them as contradictory, and de-cide to kill off all but one possibility. In this way of thinking, something must always be negated, as if our brains could only operate in a binary system. We are a house divided into winning and losing sides.

We forget that either-or is merely a mindset, a map of a particular way of viewing the territory. We become so attached to the map that we cease being able to imagine what could be beyond the edges of the paper it is printed on. Thus, in a problem situation, we lose sight of the whole of our context and focus on only one single image. It is as if we confuse God with the statue on the dashboard. Until we realize this, we live a flat existence of forced, but false choices. Until we realize this, we will cling to the rigidities of certainty, isolating ourselves from wonder and vitality.

We continually think in terms of war and opposing sports analogies when we interpret challenges as, "beating the competition" or "overcoming the opposition." Again and again, we find ourselves in factions engaged in power struggles. The people with the most authority win, like the cowboy movies of days gone by where there are always good guys and bad guys. The relationships we create, therefore, have a parent-child quality to them rather than adult-to-adult.

"I grew up to have my father's looks, my father's speech patterns, my father's opinions, and my father's posture. I also grew up with my mother's contempt for my father."
JULES PFEIFFER

FROM DOUBLE BIND TO PARADOX

"It takes two to know one."
GREGORY
BATESON

Do you remember playing with the Chinese straw finger trap puzzles when you were a child? You would slide the tip of each index finger in each end and pull with all your might, trying to get them out. The only way out of such a trap, however, is into it. A manager in a Boston electronics firm created the same kind of a verbal snare. Not realizing what he was saying, he asked an employee if she wanted to take a pay cut or work fewer hours. This is called a double bind. No matter what she said she was going to lose money.

Harvard's Chris Argyris describes this kind of crazy-making thinking as an organizational defensive routine. Some other examples from today's work place are:

- Be creative, but stay within the bounds of the norm;
- Make your own decisions, but check with others first;
- Be a team player, but excel in individual achievement;
- Take risks, but don't fail or make mistakes;
- Tell your boss the truth, but don't give your boss bad news;
- If you are going to be wrong, do it in an acceptable way;

The emotional tension that these routines produce results in minimizing, denial, defensiveness, withholding, strong-arming, and a general atmosphere of what Argyris calls, "skilled incompetence."

There is a more fluid way to think than this. As our paradigm shifts away from thinking of the world as machine and everything in it as parts, we begin to recognize its dynamic living qualities. Margaret Wheatley states, "If nothing exists independent of its relationship with something else, we can move away from our need to think of things as polar opposites."

In the tradition of Aikido, we can begin to reconcile the things we've split into oppositional forces. The word "reconcile" in its origins means to bring together again. In the same way that when you bring your two fingers closer together in that straw puzzle and find release, it is possible to shift your thinking in such a way as to make room in your mind to contain two apparently contradictory ideas, needs, or even people.

Most of us in business tend to think of stability and chaos in an either-or way. But think for a moment about the dialogue that goes on between a rocky coast and the ocean. Each is shaped by the other. Although the rocks are seen as stable, they once were lava and some day will be soil. They are always changing form. The water, which is commonly thought of as chaotic, is also the essence of stability if you consider the predictability of the tides. Both are sources of life. Both stable in different ways, both expressing chaos uniquely. The shoreline, the meeting place between either-or, is where the shift happens.

This chapter is a practice field for learning to experience the tension of opposites as a creative stretch. This stretch can break you, but rather than apart, it can break you open to a largeness and flexibility of mind capable of evoking a fluid power. The solo practices for mastering oneself translate emotional tension into creative tension by establishing an inner relationship between opposing energies. The partnered practice for developing mastery with others gives an embodied understanding of how to move from the confusion of an either-or corner to the wonder of the reflective "middle third." The group experience for expanding mastery of change focuses on developing structures of symmetry that can hold and balance organizational paradox.

"Opposites do not negate each other—they cohere in a mysterious unity and at the heart of things, they need each other—body breathing in as well as out. But we want light without darkness, spring and summer without the demands of autumn and winter. So we get glaring artificial light around the clock and beyond its borders a darkness that grows more terrifying as we try to hold it off."
PARKER PALMER

PERSONAL INTEGRITY AND PARADOX

In our culture, we prefer the ease of either-or thinking to the mystery of paradox. We seem to believe it is possible to ascend and not descend. When a growth cycle in a relationship or business shows signs of descent, we assume there is something wrong, something that has to be fixed, rather than a reflection of the cyclical nature of growth, and the need for dormancy and incubation. In paradox, opposites do not negate each other—they cohere. Just as the inhalation of our bodies needs the exhalation to sustain our health, and the light of day needs the dark of night.

Paradox breaks the polarity between logic and mystery. This is difficult for our rational minds to fathom. A metaphor can help since it demonstrates the relationship between things. Such a symbol can transfer meaning across the polarity of logic and mystery.

To do this, we'll create what some call a Mobius loop. Cut a one inch wide strip of paper six inches long. Give it a single twist and tape the ends. With a pen or pencil, begin to trace a line on the outer surface of the loop. Without lifting your pen, you will cover both sides of the entire surface meeting the beginning of your line. While there is an outer surface and an inner one, what once seemed radically opposite, can be recognized now as revealing a common space.

Now, to integrate this into your organizational life, repeat the tracing, but this time, before you start, imagine a situation in your work life where you experience two forces that seem to be contradictory or polarized. Choose one to be represented by the outer surface and the other by the inner surface. As you trace your pen around the loop this time, just wonder, without grabbing for an answer, what would

*the common space or context be that could hold them both.
Allow your mind to play with possibilities of creating a
paradoxical relationship between these polarities.*

If the loop represents the whole of our personal or organizational context, the turning place in the loop represents a complementary relationship between two opposing elements. Art students discover this when they try many colors side by side, red and blue for instance, and uncover the third dynamic aspect—purple—created out of the juxtaposition. Jazz musicians often describe a music that is separate from the sum of all the music played by individuals. People in long-term personal or professional relationships, often have a strong sense of the energy between them that is unique and different from either individual.

Robert Fritz described this as "creative tension," a force which produces a sustained sense of energy and enthusiasm and seeks resolution. While holding a clear sense of current reality and simultaneously keeping a committed sense of intent, the most natural resolution would be for the reality to move toward what we want. Think of a time when you were so excited about something you wanted to do that you couldn't wait to get out of bed in the morning. Even though you knew it would be difficult, you felt pulled forward as if by a magnet.

In contrast to this creative tension, Fritz describes emotional tension as two forces that are contradictory, moving in opposite directions, draining us of energy. An example of this "yes, but" thinking was ably described by a young banker: "I really want to take this new job—it's a phenomenal opportunity for me to learn management skills I desperately need, but I really don't think I can risk that kind of chance because I'm not very good in group situations, but . . ."

"Love is that condition in the human spirit so profound that it empowers us to develop courage; to trust that courage and build bridges with it; to trust those bridges and cross over them so we can attempt to reach each other."
MAYA ANGELOU

When you turn toward what you want, fear will, of necessity, be evoked. For those two energies are twined realities demanding a relationship. It is quite possible, however, to transform emotional tension into creative tension by "de-framing" the emotions. To do this, you have to become less interested in the story you tell yourself about either polarity and much more interested in the current reality experience of the energy of each emotion in your body. As the practices that follow demonstrate, holding them in your consciousness allows them to literally transform—to cross forms—and integrate into a new connected experience that is different than either one.

PRACTICE THIRTEEN: SOLO
Fear and Wanting

Part 1: Either/Or/Both

Begin by recalling an instance when you felt fear. It might have been a moment when you were startled in the dark, when you had a close call in a car, when you learned you had made a big mistake, or any other situation that triggered a startle response.

As you recall that moment, note the feelings in your body, which might range from a quickened heartbeat, faster respiration, clamminess, sudden numbness, and so on. Call these sensations your fear signals and note these responses for later reference.

Next, recall a moment of wanting, an instance when you felt a strong dream pulling on you. This may be related to what you experienced when you thought of your intention, the pull you felt in practice eleven as you sat in the chair.

Notice the sensations you experience in your body as you recall this moment. These may be anything from a sense of roominess and warm easing to an exciting compulsion to move, or a moment when warm tears flowed unexpectedly. Call these your signals of wanting and note them for future reference.

Now, make room in your body for both signals simultaneously. Think of both instances at the same time. What do you experience when both energies of fear and wanting are present simultaneously?

Part 2: The Middle Third

Logistics

You will need three glasses or mugs, hot tap water, and ice water.

Fill one glass with hot water (only as hot as you are comfortable immersing your hand in); fill one glass with ice water; fill the third glass halfway with ice water and halfway with hot water.

Immerse three fingers of your left hand in the hot water glass and three fingers of your right hand in the ice water glass for one minute. Now remove your fingers from the hot and cold water and immediately place both hands in the third combination glass. How do the fingers of each hand experience that water?

INTEGRATION QUESTIONS

1. What is an example of a situation at work where you have grown so accustomed to the "temperature" of your perspective that you find yourself fighting with others when a different perspective shows up? For example, do you ever hear yourself saying, "This is *the* way to do it;" "We *have* to . . . ;" "You are

[When asked if he was ever afraid] "I experience what you do. You name it fear. I name it a call to action."
MOREHEI UESHIBA, O SENSEI

wrong . . . ;" "This is my area of expertise . . . ;" "My way or the highway . . . "

2. Imagine one way you could recognize that everyone comes from a different "glass of water." How could you shift from the certainty of your belief to a centered inquiry? Can you imagine yourself saying, "What's important about that to you?" "Tell me what led you to your perspective." "This is what's important to me."

3. How do you trap yourself into proving that your opinion is the only truth? For example, do you ever hear yourself saying something like, "I'm the one getting paid to make this call, and I say our budget doesn't permit this kind exploration."

These practices do not imply that decisiveness is not valuable, but it does mean that it's important to have a greater awareness of how you are thinking. When you are soliciting new perspectives to old problems, reconsidering all possibilities with a sense of wonder is essential.

THE RIVER THAT FLOWS BETWEEN A ROCK AND A HARD PLACE

Having explored complementarity as a pathway to integrity, we move now to the bridge of reconciliation. The roots of the word mean to reestablish a friendship between, to re-create a meeting between. Quantum physicists and Aikido masters have known for quite some time that change occurs when polarities are integrated. How do you create reconciliation when two external forces pull in opposite directions?

Imagine you are the team leader of a meeting that is supposed to focus on setting priorities in a large health care system. A man and woman, the heads of two departments that have historically competed with each other for funding dollars, break into a loud argument, which goes on for ten minutes. Finally, when everyone else is coughing or rocking back and forth in their chairs, you do your best to intervene. "Now, wait a minute. You two calm down here . . . "

The man in conflict lashes back without thinking. "Why are you butting in? Who the hell do you think you are anyway?"

You are stunned and confused for a moment. You splutter and then stand up. What do you say and do next?

Between the splutter and the possible splatter comes a moment of choice. You *will* respond based on who the hell you think you are. How we relate to people is based on that definition of our identity. If you say something to yourself like, "Uh oh, things are getting out of control here. What's needed is a firm hand. I'm the leader, and that means the buck stops here. It's my job to put a stop to this," you will move from confusion to reaction, identifying yourself as the "boss."

If, on the other hand, you think something like this, "Darn! I hate fights. I've never been good in situations like this. Why should I put myself in the middle of one anyway? I'll just let them work it out and stay invisible," you will move from confusion to reaction, identifying yourself as the placator. This is a classic example of either-or thinking: Choose one of these and chances are you won't improve the situation or find the most effective solution.

To discover an alternative way of responding, consider the identities described by three wise men: Carl Jung, the psychologist, described the self as the place where opposites are integrated. Rainier Maria Rilke, the poet, described the self as "the rest between two notes always in discord." Morihei Ueshiba, the founder of Aikido, described the self as relationship,

"Work is theater, the place where life unfolds to our tragic or comic satisfaction."
DAVID WHYTE

[When asked
if he was
ever afraid]
"Yes, but I am
accustomed to
my fear."
TERRY DOBSON,
SENSEI

a non-intellectual place that can hold opposites. Each of these descriptions of an identity represents the reconciliatory aspect of the middle third. How would you respond to the conflict if you believed any one of these three, were "who the hell you thought you were?"

A way to experience this might be to find a large rubber band and slip it over your two hands so it rests around your wrists. Imagine that the rubber band represents you. As you ball each hand into a fist, you might imagine them as the two opposing forces in the above story or in a work situation of your own. Allow yourself to center and widen your senses peripherally so you achieve an expanded state of mind, moving from confusion, to curiosity, to wonder as you look at the two fists. As you explore how much slack you can take out of the rubber band, imagine you are both accepting the fists as they are and inviting them into relationship, learning from each.

If you should happen to find that one polarity seems "right" and the other "wrong," it might be worth spending some time being curious about that. What purpose could be filled by this wrongness, even if you disagree with how it is attempting to meet its needs? If we can understand in this deeper way, rather than just disowning automatically, we will be able to welcome differences as opportunities to learn to find our hidden wholeness.

This wider way of thinking makes it possible for you to hold the differences and be sensitive to them without being caught up by them. Instead of finding your bearings from polarities, you are orienting from your center. Instead of living out the fringes of who you are, you are living from your source.

In Tai Chi, this position of integrity is called "return to mountain." It can be the source of such words as, "I know each of you needs an answer right now, and I'm not ready to decide.

I wonder how we'll all reach satisfaction" or "I am not comfortable with what is happening here. I don't know what to do about it, and I don't like being this uncomfortable." It was the source of such action as Rosa Parks sitting down in the front of the bus that started the civil rights movement.

The practice that follows give you the opportunity to experience in another way how you can become a doorway, a bridge, or a reflective context for active relationship.

"Our task will be to search continuously for what is new and important, and to make sense of it in terms of who we've been and who we're trying to become."
MARGARET WHEATLEY

PRACTICE FOURTEEN: TRIAD
Double Arm Pull

Benchmark: Think of a situation at work where you seem to continually and uncomfortably get caught between two people, two opinions, two departments, and so on. This could be an ongoing situation or a one-time pressure to come to a quick decision. Write down some of the particulars including typical conversational phrases. For example, "We need you to understand that R&D needs this money more than marketing."

Logistics

Do this in groups of three. One person (person A in the middle) will practice three ways of responding to simultaneous challenges from two sources (persons B and C at each side).

Person A stands with arms hanging at his/her side (remove any watches or bracelets). Persons B and C kneel and each grasps one wrist of A. Because you deserve to learn safely and pain-lessly, A should feel free at any time to say stop to the two challengers at each wrist.

Option 1

Beginning with a signal from A to begin, persons B and C begin to pull each wrist down toward floor. In the first way of re-sponding, A attempts to be strong and stand up to or resist the two pulls.

Then, person A signals a pause and all three notice the quality of experience in relating to each other in this way. What would be a typical way that you would talk to yourself in this situa-tion? For example, "I've gotta tough this out. I'm the only one keeping this place together, so it's all up to me."

Option 2

Proceed as before except this time A will, when the pressure is applied, yield or comply to both immediately.

How would you talk to yourself in this kind of a situation? For example, "It's just too much work. It's just not worth it anymore. Why bother? We are all going down."

Option 3

This time A centers and widens his or her periphery (see practice two). When A signals for the challenge to begin, the pull can be experienced as a welcomed stretch by allowing his/her arms and joints to lengthen.

What metaphor would help A redirect the strong downward pull? For example, "The stronger the pull, the more I'll think of those hands as though they were trying to grab a greased pig, or like snow melting on bamboo, or I'll be like a snake shedding its skin."

After practicing, A signals a stop to the challenge and all three people discuss their experience. B and C then each get a chance to practice being in the center.

Benchmark Revisited: Review that situation at work which you thought about before this practice. Think of one thing you have learned here that you can apply to the situation. For example, "I learned that to not decide is an option, and that I don't have to give an answer right away." or "I've been so busy trying to handle these two guys that I had forgotten what was important to me."

INTEGRATION QUESTIONS

1. What was effective in helping A expand to contain both pulls? How did A bring him or herself into relationship with forces that seemed to be in opposition?

2. What is one instance at work where this way of being with the pulls of the current reality would be useful?

3. Think of a charged situation at work where it is too soon to decide or commit or choose. How could this practice offer you another option of response?

4. How could this practice help in the space between the impulse to act and action?

BEHAVING NORMALLY IS SOMETIMES NUTS BUT SEEKING INTEGRITY IS ALWAYS SANE

Many of the questions that haunt our organizations involve profound paradoxes such as, "How do we do more with less?" and "How do we find plenty in such scarcity?" Our habitual way of reacting to these questions is to create imbalances by manipulating situations and people so that one side—our side—wins by competing for whatever resources are available and being ignorant of the needs of the whole. As the resource of our attention becomes scarce, we even vote when we listen: "Whose opinion do I want to win? I'll ignore everyone else."

Peter Vaill, author of *Management As A Performing Art*, says that the two functions management is supposed to bring to an organization are comprehension and control of what is going on. But how do you comprehend or control paradoxes? They seem to be conflicts among apparent truths. They refuse to dissolve by normal methods of management such as getting more facts or being more logical.

Returning to Neils Bohrs' statement about how the opposite of one profound truth can be another profound truth may give us a clue. A person's healthy sense of self, for instance, ideally should be able to coexist with a capacity to act selflessly in service to others. We should be able to integrate the interior and exterior, the masculine and feminine, our intuition and our intellect, the universal and the concrete, our compassion and our wisdom, the creative and the destructive.

Parker Palmer postulates that this is so difficult because we do not create structures of symmetry to hold our paradoxes together and reflect both poles. In a major Midwestern manufacturing company, for instance, a high value was placed on design of new products, and all structures reflected this. But the balancing need—service to the needs of the "commons"— was ignored. Since most leadership ignores tension, the increasing fragmentation that was caused by this basic imbalance—resentment of designers, for example, manifesting in a we-they mentality—was also ignored. But tension continued to grow and threatened to undermine the organization as the designers became more rigid, refusing to listen to anyone

"There's an alternative. There's always a third way, and it's not a combination of the other two ways. It's a different way."
DAVID CARRADINE

else's needs or share vital information with other departments. The resolution occurred when leadership became aware of the need to support individual responsibility to the whole of the organization.

Andy Warhol, when asked how to observe a work of art, stated that it was necessary to look at it from 360 degrees. "Unfortunately, I forgot to look at my life that way," he said wryly. Unfortunately, we also forget to look at our organizations that way.

Paradoxes just sit there waiting to be contemplated. What our minds can do most effectively with them, it seems, is to reflect on them in action rather than in a fixed position. This mostly means wondering how the situation is evolving so that natural forces can work to resolve the tensions that in stop-action appear to be contradictory.

The practical challenge is not so much to transcend our limitations to resolve paradox as it is to make them more permeable. The integrity of an organization requires that we think in such a way that brings the two currents together into some sort of balance and harmony. This is not the same as compromise, which requires losing the dynamic current of each individual river. For example, you want the team to discuss priorities for funding, I want the team to discuss conflicts in communication. We end up discussing the meeting we had last week, or fighting over whose discussion should take priority. What if, instead, we acknowledged that we seemed to be going in different directions, and currently were at cross purposes? What if we inquired into what was really important to each of us? What if we wondered together how both of our needs could be met?

Thinking paradoxically requires maneuvering, not manipulation of the other. Thus, the connections between us are maintained, even when we go in different directions. It requires fostering an inward capacity for relatedness with others, with ideas, with environments. It requires a shift from information to insight, from knowledge to wisdom.

We live in an age of profound darkness and unbearable light. Some wish to re-create a past that never was, others a future that never can be. Life may appear to be doomed; life never had a better chance. Traditions are in tatters; new visions emerge from the chaos. The challenge that follows is a practiced field for expanding the ways we think as we balance on the knife's edge of our time, trying to become full citizens of a very large universe.

"You find power in the place between giving and receiving."
TERRY DOBSON, SENSEI

PRACTICE FIFTEEN: GROUP
Telephone Pole Shuffle

Logistics

You'll need a telephone pole or log that is about 12–16 feet long and resting on the ground. If prone telephone poles are not in great abundance in your city or conference room, a 2" x 6"x 16' plank from your local lumber supplier will suffice.

Work in groups of approximately 8–12 people. Position 4–6 people on each end of the pole so that the groups on either end face one another.

At a signal each group must move toward the center of the pole or plank, pass by the group going the other way, and end with all members on the other end of the log without ever stepping off the pole or 2" x 6" plank. If someone touches the ground, each group must return to their original position and begin again.

(Hint: What if you viewed the opposing team as humans sharing a scarce resource with you or as interesting acquaintances on your journey instead of as an obstacle between you and where you want to go?)

"*Many are stubborn in pursuit of the path they have chosen; few in pursuit of the goal.*"
FRIEDRICH NIETZSCHE

INTEGRATION QUESTIONS

1. What did this practice teach you about how to deal with someone who apparently is on an opposing course?

2. How did you end up sharing the precious space on the log?

3. If the log represents time or money, what did you learn about sharing those scarce resources?

4. What did you learn about creating a system that takes opposite orientations into account?

BUSINESS ANECDOTE

When practiced in a large bank, the double arm pull produced a change in the criteria used to select teams. This bank's CEO said: "We used to be careful to select members who represented the extreme polls of the population in each functional area.

"Our premise was that by including the extremes we would get an effective sampling of opinion there. Instead, we found that the representatives of the extreme poles viewed being on the team as their opportunity to garner as many gains as possible for their point of view. They defined themselves by their extreme positions and did all they could to maintain them. After the practice, we started selecting team members by their ability to flexibly and humanely entertain many different points of view. Meetings became more enjoyable and a whole lot more productive."

7

How do we get more effective results using fewer resources?

COLLABORATIVE LEADERSHIP

Moving Beyond Command and Control

"I hear people everywhere saying that the trouble with our time is that we have no great leaders any more. If we look back, we always had them. But to me it seems that there is a very profound reason why there are no great leaders anymore. It is because they are no longer needed. The message is clear. We no longer want to be lead from the outside. Each of us must be our own leader. We know enough now to follow the light that's within ourselves, and through this light we will create a new community."

LAURENS VAN DER POST

DAWNA: THE CEO'S DAUGHTER

I never heard my father say, "I love you." He said many things in his lifetime, but never that. My mother pasted newspaper clippings that chronicled his journey from an inner-city street fighter to the CEO of a major Detroit corporation. He often said he regretted never having a son, an heir to pass on the legacy of knowledge gathered as he climbed to the top of the ladder as an inspiring and commanding corporate leader.

There was one thing he didn't know, however, and it was his greatest secret and most profound shame. I remember going to his huge office after school. My feet left prints in the plush burgundy carpeting as I approached the immense mahogany desk. I pulled myself up onto the tan leather swivel chair. The only things on the shining desk top were a large reel-to-reel tape recorder, an ink blotter, and a very thick pile of papers held in place with a crystal weight that was carved with the company insignia.

Day after day, I pushed the button and began to read the papers, one by one, into the microphone. Then, when I had finished, I slipped my hand under the big black and green blotter and found the quarter my father left me so I could buy a hot fudge sundae on the way home. No one ever found out about this ritual. It was our secret. No one ever found out he couldn't read a word.

When he returned home from work every day, he put on a pair of steel-rimmed glasses and sat in a big brown wing chair with a newspaper spread wide between his hands. He moved his head back and forth in the motion most people would use to read. I slipped under the paper and crawled up on his knee to ask my inevitable question, "Daddy, do you love me?" He ruffled my hair, reached in his pocket, and whispered in my ear, "Here's a nickel, don't tell your mother."

When I was a teenager, I used to wear his huge white starched shirts over jeans to school, the sleeves rolled up, my hair in a pony tail. The biggness and stiffness never bothered me. I felt protected, surrounded in his certainty. But still, I yearned to hear those words he'd never say. The nickel became a quarter, then a dollar. After college, I stopped asking. I went into therapy, pounded on a pillow with a tennis racket, and shouted, "I hate you, I hate you, Daddy! Why won't you ever tell me you love me?" When I was full grown with a child of my own, he was saying, "Here's five dollars, don't tell your mother."

He had Alzheimer's disease for the last years of his life. That lion of a corporate commander sat shrunken and unshaven in a black rocking chair in Hollywood, Florida, staring into worlds I couldn't see. I don't know if he could have responded if he'd wanted to, but for two years there was nothing. On what turned out to be my last visit to him, I knelt down on the floor and took his face between my hands. More than anything I wanted him to know, to receive all that I felt for him. I whispered fervently, "I love you, Daddy." His watery blue eyes reflected nothing. He was locked behind walls I could not climb.

I got to my feet, slipped my purse over my shoulder, and turned away, about to leave when a thought crossed my mind. I reached into my wallet, pulled out a five dollar bill, put it in his limp hand and murmured in his ear, "Here's five dollars, don't tell Mom." Immediately he blinked, looked up at me and smiled as he said in a gentle voice, "I love you too sweetheart."

Those were the last of his words I ever heard. He returned to the place behind the walls and I went home. Still, in that one precious moment, he taught me what was perhaps the most important lesson of all.

"Giving in to get your way is the essence of Aikido," declared Sensei Terry Dobson. What that means is that we must get very close to the people we think we are in opposition to, close enough to enter their model of the world. Close enough to understand their pain, fear, and confusion.

The essence of true leadership involves removing the barriers that keep people from doing the great things they are meant to do. This may not be the commanding image we have been following in the mechanistic Newtonian era, but it can return us to the art form of influence and take us ahead to the awakening of our faith in who we can become together.

ORIENTATION

If you were swinging comfortably from a trapeze (as unlikely as this may seem) and you noticed in the distance another trapeze, *and* you noticed there was no safety net, would you be tempted to let go of the one you were holding onto? But what if you continued swinging comfortably back and forth, back and forth, and then you heard a strange sound, looked up and discovered that the ropes of the trapeze you were holding onto were unraveling rapidly from their attachment?

Almost every person living in the twentieth century has experienced more wild swings of world-shaping change than anyone since the fall of ancient Rome. This is the situation that many people in leadership positions in American business find themselves in. Recent studies show that seven out of ten mergers and acquisitions are failures. Half of all executives in target companies are dismissed or depart in less than one year. Win-lose dynamics creep into every exchange. Their language reflects the negative images: war, rapists, raiders. During such a

"When we think about leaders and the variety of gifts people bring to corporations and organizations, we see that the art of leadership lies in liberating and polishing, enabling those gifts."
MAX DEPREE

"It's not so much that we're afraid of change or in love with the old ways, but it's that place in between that we fear—it's like being between trapeezes. It's like Linus when his blanket is in the dryer— there's nothing to hold onto."
MARILYN FERGUSON

period, perception is narrowed and distorted. Disbelief, uncertainty, and anxiety are typical. Self-interest is paramount as managers find themselves vying for the top positions. This is not a climate that fosters learning new ways to reach for the next trapeze—shifting the paradigm from command and control to collaboration and innovation.

When you think about three great leaders you have known, what are their chief qualities? What metaphor would you use to describe them? Are they like the captain of a team, the general of the troops?

When a culture stands at an unprecedented frontier, there seems to arise a yearning for leaders who have the answers—especially answers we like. Technical answers, top-down solutions. But in a quantum world of such complexity as ours, planning and leading are more a matter of learning than of knowing. The shift required is from unending expansion to doing more with less, from quantity to quality, from domination to collaboration.

Believing that leaders are the people in control means that those below are *not* in control. Such a value system holds the person higher up the hierarchy as somehow a more important being. But this is a time when all hierarchies are in trouble, and organizations are calling for creativity, commitment, and innovation.

The clash between our yearning for hierarchical leadership and our need for collaborative leadership is one of our most thorny dilemmas. Peter Senge describes why this may be so: "One of the reasons the myth of the great leader is so appealing is that it absolves us of responsibility for developing leadership capacities more broadly. Viewed systemically, there is a "shifting the burden" structure in operation: A perceived need for leadership can be met through developing leadership capacities throughout the group or through relying on a hero leader. The latter reinforces a belief in the groups' own powerlessness, thus making the fundamental solution more difficult." Thus, the myths of heroes may actually block the emergence of the leadership of teams and organizations that can lead themselves.

Leadership now must mean engaging with people in facing up to essential problems—including situations where no one has the answer. This can create a paradox since authorities get rewarded for having answers and punished for saying "I don't know." Lyndon Johnson believed he couldn't afford to offer his policies up for debate. He is often quoted as saying to his aides, "Don't bring me a problem unless you have the solution." Richard Nixon also viewed public debate as a threat, preferring "the silent majority." Both enacted the old myth of leadership—the charismatic lone ranger knows the answer, where we all need to go, and how we need to get there.

Perhaps this style and model of leadership were necessary when we were driven by survival, but now we need to be driven toward what historian Arnold Toynbee called a "renewing stance, a reverence for life in order to evoke a vital awakening." Moving from a monopoly environment of operations and maintenance into a collective climate of innovation means developing a team culture that champions change and excitement.

Different capacities are necessary to shift from control to stewardship and collaborative learning. Managers who expect to secure their old sense of "power over" will be disappointed. While they will ultimately gain a new kind of instrumental power, one based on being part of a more effective, adaptable, and satisfying human system, along the way, however, they'll be

"You can no longer be the tough guy, and you also can't come on impassive, ice water in the veins, cool head. On the other hand, the kindly parent who listens and understands but does nothing approach also won't work. No, in every situation, you must lead with your real self, because if you're going to be on the leading edge of management, you sometimes must be on the emotional side as well."
JIM AUTRY

likely to experience culture shock and confusion, as when traveling in a foreign country. They may feel disoriented, disinherited and disabled.

The transformation of the outer landscape of organizations must begin with transforming the interior landscape of our minds, our mental models. Leading in permanent white water means knowing how to get our bearings in entirely new ways. We must be able to read the river. This requires knowing ourselves and our environment from a totally different perspective.

It may be that changing our images of leadership will reveal other contexts where we know how to use our influence differently, know how to listen deeply and inquire into diverse perspectives, and know how to use dissonance creatively. For example, rather than using a symphony conductor as a symbol of a leader, Max Depree, author of *Leadership Jazz* and former CEO of Herman Miller, reminds us of the vitality and power of a jazz combo "in the groove," a kind of "everybody's-in-charge," to talk of the new image of leadership. It is an image of inquiry and influence, whose magic and power rests on the interplay of the gifts of its members leading and following each other.

It's difficult to create jazz, however, if all of your training and experience is playing in a symphony orchestra. You are invited, therefore, to consider this chapter as a jam session. It offers you three sets of practices so you can find a sound that is authentically yours, learn to listen deeply to those around you in order to find a way of blending in harmony, and explore improvisation without sheet music. The solo practice for mastering oneself takes you on a kinesthetic adventure of letting go of your current style in order to organize your involvement in the whole in a more relevant way. The partnered practices for developing mastery with others gives you embodied experiences of inquiry into others' points of view and using influence effectively to assert your own. The group experience for expanding mastery of change explores composing and coordinating harmonics for the whole.

FROM COMMAND AND CONTROL TO WHAT?

Many corporate executives sense how profound a shift of mental models is being required of them. Bill O'Brien, former CEO of Hanover Insurance, who is credited with helping the company regain its momentum and become a leader in its field, describes it: "The most challenging issue is one concept that has driven managers for generations—control. In lieu of that, we have to try to create conditions under which people's internal energy or motivation can be inspired. People sense when they are treated as contributing human beings, and that treatment has a multiplying effect on their production."

Kerm Campbell, the CEO of Herman Miller, put it this way: "If you're only focused on ROI (return on investment), you'll be short-lived. Transformation will never be quantifiable. It starts with the leadership being able to navigate in the 'permanent white water' that forces us to notice the world differently."

What are the fundamentals of this new navigation? Peter Vaill says that in these conditions, the strategies of working harder and politically and technologically smarter will only take us so far. He explains, "Eventually we slam into workaholism and rudderless, isolated, striving. To maintain healthy lives as well as find the current of the river, we need to work reflectively smarter, collectively smarter, and spiritually smarter."

How do we do this? Since more and more employees have the information, autonomy, and skills to self-manage, leadership

"Example is not the main thing in influencing others—it is the only thing." ALBERT SCHWEITZER

now has to move from giving direction to setting direction, from command and control to values and vision. These become the touchstones, the guiding stars on which to set our navigation. They are not destinations, but the compass for the journey.

Iva Wilson, the CEO of Phillips Display, identifies intellectual energy and curiosity as well as a commitment to continuous personal learning as essential. "As a leader you have to commit to change yourself before you ask anyone else to do this. The most important things we carry inside ourselves. If we can center ourselves to the purpose inside, we can move forward." But leadership training programs rarely consider the internal: "I'm discouraged by how often they focus on the development of skills to manipulate the external world rather than the skills necessary to go inward, to make the inner journey," declares Parker Palmer.

What we as leaders know is now second to what we can learn. The good news is that we no longer need to walk on water. The bad news is that we have to be able to learn where the stepping-stones are.

The battles we keep encountering in our roles as leaders may reflect unfought or recurring battles within ourselves, conflicts we don't recognize or haven't dealt with. Meeting these challenges within is a beginning point for meeting the challenges around us.

DOING MORE WITH LESS: LEARNING TO SERVE

The skills a martial arts master and a transformational leader must learn are, in essence, the same: to be calm under pressure; to maintain balanced power; to perceive the whole; to

"There go my people. I must find out where they are going so that I can lead them."
ALEXANDRE LEDRU-ROLLIN (French politician)

"To lead the people, walk behind them."
LAO TZU

concentrate; to concentrate the energy of others; and to direct the forces around them to positive ends.

The literal meaning of *samurai* is one who serves, and an essential shift in identity that leaders must learn to make is from being the Lone Ranger to becoming part of a larger whole. A servant leader is a practical idealist, committed to the dignity and self-worth of all the people in an organization. She or he believes that power flows *from* those people. Pragmatically, we know from the military that the only officer that soldiers will follow is one who is both competent and committed to the well-being of those led.

Structured for success, most of us have spent a lifetime carving security out of what we know and what we can control. Our belief that power equals control is the equation that is the most limiting. We rarely consider on what our strength is based. Try this little experiment:

Touch the tips of your thumb and forefinger together in an OK gesture. Ask another person to hook both of their forefingers into the ring made by your fingers, and try to pull it open. The chances are that the strength of their two arms overpower that of your two fingers.

Use less to do more. Shake out your hands and form the OK gesture again, but this time touch your fingertips to each other very lightly and use your mind to help—imagine your fingers form a solid metal ring.

Ask your partner to again put two forefingers between the ring and pull, but gradually increasing the force from gentle to full. You absorb the pull, rather than resisting it.

Most people find that they can maintain the iron ring even against someone who is stronger in the conventional sense.

"The best way for leaders to get visions across to people is to live it themselves.
EDWIN LOCKE

Surrendering to an image of the whole makes it possible to do more with less.

The first kind of strength, which most people use to control situations or other people is a combination of physical force, knowledge, and experience. Koichi Tohei, the founder of Ki Aikido, likens this to the visible segment of an iceberg. Below the surface, however, where the whole of the iceberg exists, is a vast potential, which, if we are able to tap into it, can increase our life power manyfold. That unseen portion is the mind and spirit. When we unify them with our bodies, we begin to utilize that energy.

The first way you created the ring was with force, which is the essence of authority. The second was with a kind of power that emanates from surrender and sensitivity, that yields a whole new context of options. This can be essential to new mental model of leadership. By becoming sensitive to how you hold on, you can let go.

A boss who uses authority to make sure employees work harder will achieve results *until* he or she goes on vacation or off-guard. When, on the other hand, the boss reorients to a more proportional involvement by inviting other members of the system to share in the function of allocation of responsibility, the essence of efficient coordination occurs.

Ruth Alon, a gifted and brilliant teacher of psychophysical reeducation calls this fundamental principle "functional integrity." The practice that follows is an adaptation of one she uses to help people relieve the pain in their necks. She calls it, appropriately enough, "sending the boss on vacation while the business is still going on." If the head can be thought of as the boss, giving orders, and the body as the workers, carrying out the orders, then the neck is responsible for negotiating the

"How can I be a leader I want to follow?"
JANE LAPOINTE

"It is like I have to live in two worlds—the old world of control and domination and the new world of learning. I know that the new world is what's needed, but I am so capable in the old world."
ANONYMOUS

relationship between the two. Its muscles are often involved way beyond what the normal function requires. This is how tension is exaggerated.

When these muscles are inhibited, as occurs in this practice, the boss is sent on vacation to let go of tensions and figure out other ways of being involved. Consequently, the nervous system has the opportunity to operate through other avenues that might not carry the old prejudices about how hard it is to move the neck. When the old way is inhibited, the pain in the neck can disappear and a new quality of ease and coordinated efficiency can emerge. On the level of the body *and* the organization, this is a revolution!

PRACTICE SIXTEEN: SOLO
Boss on Vacation

Logistics
You might want to tape this practice slowly and then play it back and follow your own instructions. Another way would be to read a paragraph or two, do it, read, do it, and so on.

Sitting comfortably in a chair allow your eyes to close. Bring awareness to your neck. In your mind's eye notice how your neck is shaped, the length, diameter, width. What are its various angles and degrees of extension? Sense your neck's different parts: your skin, your vertebrae, your deeper tissues, your muscles, the fluids and pulses within. Use your hands to explore the tissues of your neck for a few minutes.
Begin turning your head to the right and then bring it

"Talks of leadership come from the heart: listen. In every office you hear the threads of love and joy and fear and guilt, the cries for celebration and reassurance, and somehow you know that connecting these threads is what you are supposed to do and business takes care of itself."
JIM AUTRY

back to the front. Repeat this small movement very softly several times. Check how far your head goes to the right. Notice your range of ease. Do a little less than you are able.

Notice the angle of your rotation by picking out some point on the wall. Slowly rotate your head to the left and explore your range of motion and ease on this side. Notice how you can respect the signals of discomfort that your body communicates to you and not push beyond them. Acknowledge the range that is natural for you when you keep the movement soft and smooth.

Compare moving in both directions and notice which side is more restricted. On the basis of that exploration, choose one side to support and improve for today. Bring your awareness to your neck on that learning side by touching it with the opposite hand.

Then let go with that touching hand, and let it follow a trail across your chest until it comes to rest naturally in the palm of the other hand. While the elbow of the touching hand hangs lazily and heavily, you can begin to carry that hand once again closer to your learning neck and shoulder. Let it rest there. The other hand can slowly drop down across your chest.

You can support the elbow of your touching hand with the palm of your other hand, thus creating a scaffolding that minimizes the need for effort throughout your system. In that position, take a few minutes to allow your fingers to explore the area between your neck and shoulder on your learning side. This is the area that connects your head to the rest of your body. Let your fingers gently notice any place of tightness or conflict between muscles. Let your eyes close and open when they like, breathing softly and deeply.

Let the palm of your touching hand select a spot on your learning shoulder. Begin to collect the muscle tissues into your palm until you can hold them by squeezing gently. Turn your head away from your squeezing hand, and then bring it back toward it. Continue this back and forth motion for a few minutes gradually decreasing the motion and effort until you reduce it by 50 percent of what you know you are capable of doing. Make a mental note about how smoothly your neck can travel within that range.

Repeat several cycles of this moving exploration while gripping your muscle. Rest your hand by letting go of the grip for a few long soft breaths and close your eyes to notice the sensations where you have just been touching.

Once again carry your touching hand to your learning shoulder and neck. Trust that your fingers will be drawn to an area that is meaningful for you. When your palm is wrapped around some tissue move your head and neck in space in a random way, without pattern. Let your jaw be loose.

After a period of time, pause in your explorations and let your hand return to rest in your lap while you take some slow breaths and notice the sensations in your body. Rotate your neck side to side once again and note its range of motion as compared to the first time you made that benchmark.

INTEGRATION QUESTIONS

1. How could/did you make the shift from controlling your neck through effort and force to being curious, doing less, and relaxing?

2. How did the muscles under your squeezing hand respond to being brought to a full stop and letting your other muscles take responsibility?

3. What is one situation at work where you have supplied the momentum or control around a project or effort? What would it be like for you to step back and invite a broader examination of the process?

WOULD YOU RATHER BE RIGHT OR EFFECTIVE?

A CEO of a major Midwestern manufacturing company put it this way: "I know I have to change my leadership style, but I just don't feel very safe making myself vulnerable to the people I work with, especially the ones with titles! The truth is, I don't know what real collaboration *feels* like. This may sound dumb, but how do you *do* it?"

As far as we can ascertain, there's not one single course in any major business school on collaborative skills. A young man about to receive his MBA degree, described it as a "Master in Bossing Around." Leadership skills are commonly thought to be very similar to those of a coach of a baseball team. So, for the CEO brave enough to speak the truth about his skilled incompetence, for the new MBA, and for any of you who are not suffering from hardening of the attitudes with BTDT (been there, done that), here is a potent description of the feel of collaboration by a master in the unknown—jazz musician, Stephen Nachmanovitch:

"I play with my partner. We listen to each other. We mirror each other; we connect with what we hear. We anticipate, sense, follow, and lead each other. We open each other's minds like an infinite series of Chinese boxes. A mysterious kind of information flows back and forth, quicker than any signal we might give by sight or sound. The work comes from neither one of us, even though our own idiosyncrasies and styles, the symptoms of our original natures, still exert their natural pull. Nor does the work come from a compromise or halfway point (averages are always boring!), but from a third place that isn't necessarily like what either one of us would do individually. What comes is a revelation to both of us."

"Leaders should lead as far as they can and then vanish. Their ashes should not choke the fire they have lit."
H. G. WELLS

Obviously, a new set of competencies is required that are consistent with the choice to belong to a mutual, open, inquiring system, but this doesn't mean that we have to go out and start from scratch. Our very essence is an example of this kind of collaborative creation; in genetics, it's called the law of requisite variety, which simply means that when we cross one variety with another, we multiply the variety of the total system. Without that collaborative meshing of genes, we'd still all be protozoa or slime molds, the full riches of evolution would not be possible, and none of us would be worrying about shifting paradigms!

Collaborative leadership requires a discipline of increased awareness, sensitivity, consideration, listening, and willingness to be subtle. The art is learning to trust yourself with someone else, which can seem to be a gigantic risk at first, and it leads to the even more challenging risk of encouraging other people to learn how to trust themselves with you.

A familiar example is inherent in being a baseball team member. For a minute, shift your thinking from leadership as in the coach of the team to leadership as in the whole team itself. The commerce of communication on the field is catching and throwing a ball. In order to do this, you use the most basic skills required for collaboration. Keep your periphery as wide as possible, go for the ball when it's hit near you, and, instead of catching the ball with a stiff arm, allow your mitt to absorb and follow the direction of the ball before shifting it to your other hand and throwing it in the direction you want it to go. Again, it's not at all a matter of meeting halfway or compromise, which most people misunderstand as the basis for good leadership.

"In the martial experience, you learn that it's very good to be close to your opponent. When I'm close to him, I know exactly where he is, what he's thinking, what he's likely to do. I can control, direct, relax, quiet, and restore this person by being close to him."
TERRY DOBSON, SENSEI

BLENDING: USING INQUIRY AND INFLUENCE

The old bridge in business partnerships used to be the contract. The new one is the relationship. The old skills used to be dependence and codependence; the new ones are receptivity and connection, inquiry and influence. In Aikido, this is called non-resistance. *Ai* means to harmonize, to meet, to come into agreement with. *Ki* means energy. *Do* is the way to do that— the way to harmonize energetically. This means not opposing that which is—a situation, your feelings about a situation, or other people's feelings about a situation, but acknowledging it instead in order to understand. It does not mean, however, lying down on the field and letting some other player run spiked shoes over your face.

Aikido masters say that opposing an attack directly feeds it. You may stop the other person temporarily. But, you don't stop his or her intention to attack. In Aikido, instead of opposing, you transform the energy. To do this, you must honor it, blend with it, and cocreate an outcome at a higher level of relationship than previously existed.

When someone rushes at you, rather than opposing the force (standing in the line of attack), you first position yourself by stepping off the line from the oncoming energy. Instead of being pushed over or pushing back against, you join the flow of the energy by entering in closely to the other person, turning and facing the direction he or she is facing, and try to understand that viewpoint. In this way, we open a doorway to bring the other person around in our direction. Management guru Steven Covey puts it this way, "Seek first to understand, then to be understood."

This emphasizes the principle that Parker Palmer identifies with the words, "presume collaboration." A person who ap-

"Aggression depends on duality: there must be a you and a me. If when I attack you, you become similar to me, you are hard to locate and therefore hard to attack. This is what is meant by blending. You become like the person attacking you and he or she has no place to focus aggression."
WENDY PALMER,
SENSEI

pears to be in opposition is thought of as a partner who is giving us the gift of incoming energy to work with. As the situation unfolds, we enter into an inquiry. Whether they approach with anger, frustration, enjoyment, sadness, fear, a contrasting view, or a dissonant opinion, we don't oppose them. Instead we make ourselves safe enough to inquire as to what is going on, what the person's reasoning is, what his or her needs are, why she or he feels that way, and what the primary intention is.

This increases the possibility that there will be a flexing, a bending, a willingness on the part of the other person. At this point, we listen for the opening to influence, the opportunity to lead the interaction so the other may come around and explore our point of view. Martial artists and master leaders influence by leading people's attention, sensitively drawing them into the space you want by helping them to what they are already moving toward.

Both inquiry and influence require an aware sensitivity. Inquiry implies a willingness to be sensitive to the missing or dissident voice. Certain Native Americans, according to Paula Underwood, author and teacher, frequently ask the question, "Who speaks for wolf?" This is a request for someone to speak the lone voice, the unpopular opinion or unasked question, that may in fact, hold the essential kernel of missing truth.

Inquiry also requires an awareness of the effect something is having on you, and the effect you are having on someone else. If you notice a person is cringing and stepping back from you, then whether you are right or not is immaterial. What is essential is to notice that and consider whether that's the effect you want to have.

Likewise, influence is used here instead of the word *leverage*, which is commonly used in business today. The latter is

> *"In place of tiny billiard balls moved around by contact forces, there are what amount to so many patterns of active relationship."*
> DANA ZOHAR

appropriate for machines, but implies a kind of force that is less effective in collaborative relationships. A living system is moved through influence. Controlling less allows people room to do more. Rather than motivating someone by trying to find the leverage that gets them to do what you want them to do, think about how you could encourage the factors that would help them to motivate themselves. For example, a utilities firm that had to downsize offered educational grants to employees willing to be trained in new technologies.

> *To practice using your influence sensitively, find a heavy door that opens outward. Experiment to discover where to push so you can get maximum effect from your body using the least effort. Try touching the door with your little finger or the edge of your hand and sidestep to push rather than falling into it.*

IF ANYONE LOSES, EVERYONE LOSES

Relating in this nonresistant way puts us in a position to create together, with no force lost to friction or opposition. All our attention is focused on learning together, generating solutions and creating positive action. This may mean, for example, something as simple as getting close to the other person by sitting in a nonthreatening location or walking together side by side. This has been called "the proximity principle." It says that the closer you are to the source of a force, the stronger your power will be. In other words, closeness increases influence, distance diminishes it. Tom Peters gave an example of this when he talked about "managing by walking around."

Often, when people first learn about this flexible way of relating, they say, "Well, why should I be the first one to yield, why should I bend before the other?" Sensei Richard Kuboyama's answer to that question was, "Because you are privileged to have this learning about flexibility. Others are not so fortunate. Therefore, it is your responsibility to teach them this wonderful lesson of nonresistant leading."

If you are not willing to be moved by a situation or a person, then your current reality is that you don't wish to engage effectively. This is fine. Sometimes, you may find yourself in the outfield when you want to be on a putting green. Be nonresistant with yourself: Inquire as to what you need in the moment; What your intention really is; What's important to you. Then redirect your attention to something else that may increase your sensitivity.

Some people still equate the word "sensitive" with weak. Does softening the rigidities within us really produce a diminishment of power? The practices that follow ask you to take a risk and discover from your own experience if this is so.

"It is a terrible thing to look over your shoulder when you are trying to lead—and find no one there."
FRANKLIN DELANO ROOSEVELT

PRACTICE SEVENTEEN: PAIR
Relating Instead of Controlling

Benchmark: Think about a time at work when your best efforts to advocate for an idea or to influence someone were met with a backlash, resistance, or a sense of wasted effort. Jot down a few details regarding the situation for later reference.

Part 1
Butterfly on Wrist

Person A extends one arm with a closed fist. Person B grasps A's wrist as shown in the photo.

For a minute B attempts to move or steer A's arm in any direction. A does all possible to keep from being moved.

After one minute of effort both people pause and note the effects of relating to one another in this fashion. What is a phrase or metaphor that comes to mind? For example: close-minded, resistant, pushy, insensitive, heavy-handed, adversarial, controlling, manipulative, "like a bulldozer pushing a boulder."

Person A begins as before by extending an arm and again makes a great effort not to be swayed from this position. This time B centers as described in chapter two. With great awareness very lightly, like a butterfly landing on a branch, makes contact with A's wrist.

After making contact B feels or "listens" for the motion that already exists in A's arm. Because A is alive, there is always motion in his/her arm even if it is very slight. B senses the energy in motion in A's arm and then follows it, joins it, and influences by amplifying it until the two hands move together without clashing or forcing in a motion previously unconceived by either one.

Moving together in such a fashion B can notice where opportunities exist to lead A's arm in the original direction. Person B can notice how there might be a million paths to get to that direction rather than the one initially attempted: some of which lead to struggle, some of which lead to harmony and relationship with A by extending, leading, following.

After a minute of relating in the butterfly fashion, both people pause and notice the effects of this second way of relating. What is a phrase or metaphor that describes it?

INTEGRATION QUESTIONS

1. What if butterfly-on-wrist were a working physical definition of inquiry and influence?

2. How would you "sell" an idea, initiative, or program which you fervently believed in if you used the butterfly approach as your guide?

3. From a systemic view, what is the relative efficiency of each approach? How would you sketch the energetic vectors of the two different ways of relating?

4. What mental models or stories are revealed in each approach?

Part 2
Blending

In this practice you can apply what you learned from the butterfly-on-wrist to a full body practice. Persons A and B configure themselves as shown in the photograph.

Option 1

Person B (in the dark shirt in photo) begins to push against A's hand (light shirt). A's first and perhaps instinctual response is to meet force with force by pushing back against B's hand.

Both A and B take a moment to notice the effects of this way of relating and any stories associated with it. For example, "I've got to be forceful to get my fair share of this quarter's budget."

Option 2

A second response to B's push could be collapse or acquiescence, as shown in the following photo.

Both A and B take a moment to notice the effect of this outcome and any stories associated with it. For example, "This guy's got the most clout . . . no use fighting him."

Option 3

Blending is an option beyond struggle and collapse. Person A centers as described in chapter 2. Then B begins to push as before. As the push begins A can practice his/her ability to be flexible and to turn like a revolving door. While staying close to B without being run over, A can come to know B's direction and strengths and also sense moments when B's direction and speed can be influenced.

Person B may notice a sense of being momentarily caught off-balance and confused when A turns. Instead of using that imbalance to cause harm, Aikidoist Terry Dobson taught that A should lead B back to safe balance, thus respecting the right and privilege of B's feelings while, at the same time, protecting his/her own rights and privileges. In that close and harmonious contact, A is free to take B to another perspective or let B go on his/her own way.

Persons A and B then take a moment to notice the effects of being together in this fashion. What is a phrase or metaphor that describes the contact? An example could be, "using the energy like a sailor charting a course through the wind."

Benchmark Revisited: Return to the original situation that you noted before you practiced butterfly-on-wrist and blending. What is one learning you could transfer from these practices to the situation that you noted in the beginning?

INTEGRATION QUESTIONS

1. In the absence of controlled efforts to direct, what is the nature of the relationship that develops between A and B?

2. How does A need to think to foster curiosity instead of certainty about B's push?

3. From a systemic view, what is the relative efficiency of each response? How would you draw the energetic vectors of each response?

4. As you practice, what mental models or stories are revealed in each response?

5. Which response leaves you the most free to maneuver? the most stuck without options?

6. Observe your usual style of dealing with conflict. When or with whom is that style not effective? When or with whom is it effective?

7. Under what conditions will you allow yourself to be influenced?

FLOCKING: THE TEAM AS LEADER

The world now requires leadership with a qualitative change in perspective. EDS has made its top priority leadership. They don't call it *leadership development,* rather it is termed *leadership unlocking.* Jim Young, assistant to the chairman, describes this shift: "We're moving from a world where there are continual leaders and continual followers to one where all people must periodically lead and follow. Leadership is required throughout the whole organization. Any one of us is sometimes a leader and sometimes a follower—it depends on the task, and we need to flow seamlessly between these roles."

If you have been raised in the American culture, you floated in an embryonic sac of competitiveness. Young people are influenced to think that they must win to achieve a feeling of competence. The problem is that a purely competitive system produces winners and losers. While winning produces competence, competition also can foster a crippling fear of failure. And although the shelves are jammed with books on every aspect of leadership, we have not found one on the skills of followership.

"Adversity reveals genius; prosperity conceals it."
HORACE

If an organization is, in essence, a community whose context is dependent on collaborative relationships, how can it be led and followed? How do we give in just enough so we can move as a system? How do we support people working effectively together in teams?

Turning to a dynamic in nature—the example of migrating geese may yield some clues. Robert MacNeish, assistant superintendent of the Baltimore public schools put it this way: "As each bird flaps its wings, it creates an "uplift" for the bird following. By flying in a V formation, the whole flock adds 71 percent greater flying range than if each bird flew alone."

Whenever a goose falls out of formation, it suddenly feels the drag and resistance of trying to fly alone. Quickly it gets back into formation to take advantage of the "lifting power" of the bird immediately in front. When the lead goose gets tired, it rotates back into the formation and another goose flies at the point position. The geese in formation honk from behind to encourage those up front to keep up their speed. When a goose gets sick or wounded or shot down, two geese drop out of formation to follow it down and help and protect it. They stay with it until it's either able to fly again or dies. Then they launch out on their own with another formation or catch up with their flock.

"Learning is not something added, but a reorganization of what already is."
MILTON ERICKSON

BALANCING AUTONOMY AND CONNECTION

Unlike the geese, we seem to have difficulty learning to function in teams because we're all running in different directions, trying to win the inevitable race against what?—The clock? The other company? Ourselves? How can we win together? How can we strive together—which is the original meaning of the word *competition?*

Margaret Wheatley reminds us there are no answers to these questions: "The dance of the universe extends to all the relationships we have. Knowing the steps ahead of time is not important; being willing to engage with the music and move freely onto the dance floor is what's key."

Rather than trying to understand this dance in a mechanistic way, let's uncover some of the emergent patterns and elements of the web of kinship that are the essence of an interdependent learning community. Leaders may play a crucial role in selecting the melody, setting the tempo, establishing the key, and mobilizing the energy of the players, but the music comes from something that can not be directed—from a unified whole created among the individual players.

Let's return for a moment to the musical metaphor to understand how this would work: Every note has its own place and every tone interrelates with every other. When do sounds equal music? When each answers a question posed by some other sound in the total group, when each larger grouping of sounds both questions and answers the field of thought and emotion in the listeners and players. Music has unity and intricate diversity, economy, completeness, compactness, and open-endedness.

Harmony, which we all seem to seek in both organizations and music, is actually the weaving together of dissonance with consonance. The latter generates movement in music; it gives dynamism. Most Western music focuses on consonance, but in many other cultures, such as in Bali or the Orient, there is a focus on polyrhythms or dissonance. Certain instruments, the gongs in Java, for example, set the pulse, the constancy. They ground the dissonance so the tension it creates can be used to move forward.

What if the emerging role of leadership in our increasingly diverse and "polyrhythmic" organizations were that of the gong or drum? To maintain balance in the music, you must have a reference point, a way to be true to yourself, and bearings to lead yourself home when you're lost in the chaos and cacophony of the community. This is the gong or drum—a clear core of values, a felt sense of centered intent.

Leadership that facilitates connection uses values and vision as a grounding and reference point and holds it in current reality by setting the overall basic rhythm that helps individuals know where they are in the current reality. Dee Hock, the founder of Visa, describes the importance of this: "Since the strength of any organization lies in the sense of community of the people attracted to it, its success has much more to do with the clarity of a shared vision, common principles, and strength of belief, than with assets, expertise, operating ability, or management competence, important though these may be. Businesses die out, not when they are defeated or suppressed, but when they become despairing and lose excitement about the future."

In addition to keeping the beat, the leadership of collaboration also needs to sense the overall energy flow of an organization, modify conditions which block it, notice where there are openings, and assist individuals in bringing forth their own unique capacities. The spaces between the notes, the rests in the place where the music is born, are an integral element in the music. These places and times when vision is lacking can be used to notice current reality rather than merely "visioning harder." Taking an accurate stock of what is and sharing the

"In the beginner's mind there are many possibilities. In the expert's mind, very few."
SHUNRUYU SUZUKI

truth of the present moment, often creates the balance and quiet necessary for the music to be born.

The practice that follows is an experimental field for supporting the incubation of the essentials of autonomy, connection, inquiry, influence, blending, and perhaps even a migration toward the warmth and sense of belonging that a community committed to learning can provide. Whole new kinds of human relationships and fresh harmonies are possible in a structure where rules are not dictated by authority but created by the players. Collaboration can be, in and of itself, the expression of, the vehicle for, and the stimulus to the music we can call learning communities.

"Because the relationship between self and the world is reciprocal, it is not a question of first transforming your life and then acting in the world. As you care enough to live boldly, the world will act through you."
JOANNA MACY

PRACTICE EIGHTEEN: GROUP
Community Instead of Collision

Option 1

Leader as Tent Pole

Logistics
You will need at least seven people.

- ⑤ Begin by creating a circular configuration of at least six people with one more person standing in the middle. This one person represents the command and control leader analogous to the tent pole which holds up the big top.

- ⑤ Each person in the circle imagines his/her intention as a target existing at a point directly across the circle from where he/she is standing.

⑥ At a signal given by the leader, one person walks toward his/her target, passing through the point where the leader stands in the center. Each of the outside people randomly takes their turn to move toward his/her destination in a very quick sequence but not simultaneously.

⑥ The leader's job is to direct traffic and make sure that each person gets to his or her target on the other side.

⑥ After each person has reached their destination, everyone pauses to notice the effects of "moving toward their vision" in this fashion, and describes the quality of contacts that occurred as each person move along their path. Make sure that the leader has a chance to describe the experience of being in the center.

Option 2

Leader Blending with Encounters

In this second round, reconfigure as above, but before starting, the leader will bring to mind the skills from the centering practice, as well as the butterfly, blending, and telephone pole shuffle practices. The leader might also find a metaphoric question useful, such as, "How could I enjoy dancing with all these people instead of working so hard to manage them?"

Then once again the leader signals to begin the random but sequential crossing of each person in the outside circle. This time the leader can be aware of the maneuvering space between people and make helpful, respectful contact with each person. The rest of the participants will also have the chance to blend when they encounter someone en route to their target.

After each person has arrived at their goal, everyone pauses and notices the quality of their journey during this second attempt. Describe the quality of contact in the chance meetings, interchanges, and collisions that occurred as each person moved along their job path. Again, make sure that the leader has a chance to describe the experience of being in the center.

INTEGRATION QUESTIONS

1. What is one thing you learned from this practice about keeping a sense of our own values and balance while deeply receiving another point of view?

2. Describe your attitude toward the people you met in the different parts of the practice.

3. Under what conditions will you allow yourself to listen or be influenced by another?

BUSINESS ANECDOTE

A vice president of a global manufacturing company describes how practice seventeen worked for her: "One day an employee walked into my office obviously ready for a fight. His expression was one of someone going into battle. He sat on the edge of his chair and leaned aggressively toward me. As you can imagine, I positioned myself for a fight. George began by saying that he had been with the company for eight months, had been working at a level which was higher than he was hired in, and felt he deserved an upgrade and a raise.

"I immediately told him he was hired according to the skills he had and what the job required. I let him know how survey data supported that he was not only graded correctly, but definitely paid fairly. He, of course, stated that he felt he was not totally appreciated for what he was doing. I said I was sorry he felt that way, because we did appreciate what he did—end of conversation. As he walked out of my office, shoulders slumped, I had this sick feeling in my stomach. I couldn't exactly pinpoint why I felt bad, after all, I had given him the facts and they were true. As I sat and thought about the conversation, the practice about blending flew into my mind. There's nothing quite like knowing you blew it.

"The next day I called George back into my office and had another conversation. Blending never left my mind. As I casually touched George's shoulder, I gently walked around to his side, kind of like a square-dance move, and said this: 'George, I did not feel good about our conversation yesterday. I want to have it again, because I have been thinking about how you are feeling. You are right, you have been doing an excellent job, everyone comments on it. I have been happy with the way you deal with customers. What I failed to explain to you is the way our jobs are graded and how our salaries are positioned.'

"I, then, explained to him that we grade our jobs on survey information, and that salaries are recommended and approved based on this basis. The job he was doing was completely within the position, description, and salary comparable with the other employees doing the same type of job. I also talked about his upcoming performance appraisal and merit increase that would impact his salary. We explored the other opportunities that he might consider within the organization and what he might have to do to qualify for these positions.

"What was strange was, the contractual outcome of this

"When a dog runs at you, whistle for him." THOREAU

meeting was the same. There would be no promotion or salary increase, but he left feeling more informed and comfortable about why a decision had been made. He also applied for another position within his department and received it. What a simple thing to do. It seemed like a dance . . . very flowing and easy for both of us."

"I will live with my bareness out of view. Only then will I dare to walk as a chief."
RUTH BEEBE

COLLABORATIVE LEADERSHIP INVOLVES:

- being open to perceive new ideas;

- allowing oneself to be moved by others' opinions;

- creating new alternatives;

- redirecting aggressive action into mutual collaboration;

- sensing the intentions beneath actions;

- separating people from problems and issues;

- sensing a crisis before it occurs;

- staying centered in your core beliefs, while making room for others';

- being at full power without interfering with others;

- leading interactions and extending relationships;

- generating mutual win-win solutions.

8

How do we perceive the whole in business instead of just thinking about how we can survive individually?

THE WE OF I

Acting Systemically

To those who have the heart to seek a new path . . . it is a path based on reflecting on our deepest aspirations, honoring personal visions and conversation, being more intelligent together than we can ever be separately. It is a path based on the primacy of the whole rather than the primacy of the parts. It is a path fundamentally different from the path along which industrial development in the West has progressed."

PETER SENGE

WALKING FROM THE HEART OF CONNECTION

adapted from a factual story told by Jack Kornfield in *A Path With Heart*

Following the death of Mahatma Gandhi, a number of his followers wanted to have a gathering to discuss how best to continue his work. They wanted Vinoba Bhave, Ghandi's closest disciple to lead this conference. He declined at first, but finally agreed on the condition that it could be postponed for six months, long enough for him to walk on foot from where he lived to the meeting, halfway across India.

He began to walk from village to village. In the first, he called a meeting as Gandhi had done. Many of the people were very poor, and he listened to their tales of hardship and hunger. He asked them why they didn't grow their own food, but most were of the Untouchable caste and had no land. After meditating on this, Vinoba promised that when he returned to Delhi, he would speak to Prime Minister Nehru to see if a law could be passed giving land to the poorest villagers in India.

That night, Vinoba could not rest. In the morning, he called the villagers together to apologize. "I know government too well," he said, "Even if after several years I'm able to convince them to pass a law granting land, you may never see it. It will go through the states and provinces, the district head man and the village head man, and by the time the land grant reaches you, with everyone in the government taking their piece, there probably will be nothing left for you."

One rich villager stood up and said, "I have land. How much do these people need?" There were sixteen families, each needing five acres apiece, so Vinoba said, "Eighty acres," and the man, deeply inspired by the spirit of Gandhi and Vinoba, offered eighty acres. Vinoba replied, "No, we cannot accept it. You must first go home and speak with

*your wife and children who will inherit your land." The man
did this and returned saying, "Yes, we will give eighty acres
of our land."*

*The next day, Vinoba walked to another poor village and
heard the plight of hunger and landlessness from its lowest
caste members. In the meeting, he recited the tale of the
previous village, and another rich landowner was inspired
from the story. He offered one hundred and ten acres for
the desperate twenty-two poorest families and again was
directed to get permission from his family. Within the day,
the land was granted to the poor.*

*Village by village, Vinoba held meetings and continued
this process until he reached the council several months
later. In the course of his walk, he collected over twenty-two
hundred acres of land for the poorest families along the way.
He told this story to the council, and from it, many joined
him to start the great Indian Land Reform Movement. For
the following fourteen years, Vinoba Bhave and thousands of
those inspired by him walked through every state, province,
and district of India, and without any government complica-
tions or red tape, collected over ten million acres of land for
the hungriest and most impoverished villagers.*

This entire movement began with a shift in thinking. One man
had the willingness to broaden his perspective, to drop everything he knew until he could be as a beginner again, a child of
wonder with the willingness to listen to what is, the simplicity
to see what life asks of us with unclouded eyes, and the great
heart of one who cares about all of humanity.

Oppression is not simply the result of mindless external
forces; it comes also from the fact that we collaborate with
these forces, granting consent to the very thing that is crushing
our spirit. Vinoba teaches us that when we perceive the systemic nature of our world, we cease being victims or specta-

tors, and we can be directly involved in the making of the world and ourselves. Empowered by the community, we can translate "private problems" into opportunities for cultural change.

ORIENTATION

What holds an organization together? What is its basic connective tissue? If we are to think about these questions objectively, analytically, we will stand outside of them using what author Morris Berman calls "non-participating" consciousness—we, in here, think about "it," out there. The organization becomes a thing to be measured, manipulated, and controlled. It loses meaning, spiritual purpose. In 1927, physicist Werner Heisenberg's great discovery was that there was no such thing as an independent observer. Objectivity, separation, and isolation are myths. There's no there "out there."

In spite of this, most of us still do not function from a participatory consciousness. Several years ago, a study was done by the Carnegie Institute with graduate business students who were asked their opinion of the future of the world. Eighty percent said they thought it was in a rapid decline, "going to hell in a handbasket." When asked about their own future, however, the same students thought it would be quite positive—since they had a good education, they would get a good job, make a good living, and so on. They thought of their personal autobiographies as separate from the life story of the world, as if they could carve little parts of the world away and live in them.

It has been said that what we in the West bring to the world is a capacity for fostering individual ingenuity and action; what the East brings is the capacity for fostering connectedness; what the indigenous peoples bring is a capacity for

"The notion that all these fragments are separately existent is evidently an illusion and this illusion cannot do other than lead to endless conflict and confusion."
DAVID BOHM

fostering understanding of the natural world. Peter Senge, in the introduction to the Chinese version of *The Fifth Discipline*, describes the evolution of the first two different cultural ways of thinking: "We in the West see a world composed of things, while you see a world of processes. We act individually, while you are still tied to family and community. We believe in simple cause and effect, and continually search for the all-encompassing "answer," while you tend to reason from concrete particulars, and seek more to understand the web of interdependencies within which such action must be taken. We think in days and months, while you think in decades and generations. For us, time is an adversary, while, I believe, for you it is more of an ally."

"People should walk down the street as if they belonged to each other."
ETTIENNE DECROIX

The forces of fragmentation that came with industrialization have created the organizational incoherence we now find ourselves in, as well as contributed to rigid thinking patterns, over-competitiveness, and reactiveness, which are at the core of many of today's problems. An engineer in a major automobile company described a typical example: He and his team were to design a transmission for a new model car. They had virtually no contact with the other designers of the rest of the car, and tried to finish ahead of the other teams. When the transmission was installed, it caused the car to vibrate so intensely that it shook it to pieces.

Clearly we've been on the wrong track, but how do we shift to participating consciousness? What do we have to do to reclaim what Parker Palmer calls our inward capacity for relatedness? We need to embrace the guiding ideas of connectedness, and of the primacy of the whole. We need to think about systems whose elements hang together because they continuously affect one another over time and operate toward a common purpose. To understand a system, we need to understand how it fits into a larger system. As Russell Ackoff states, "We will never understand why standard cars have seats for four or five if we look at the physical properties of its elements. To understand the car design, we need to see how it fits into a society of families who travel together."

Michael Goodman of Innovation Associates states that a Systems Thinker is someone who can observe four levels operating simultaneously: the event, the pattern of behavior or trend, the ways that trends influence each other, and the mental models or beliefs that are in operation. If you're visiting a relative and the water in your morning shower suddenly becomes scalding, habitually, you'd quickly try to turn up the cold water. Thinking systemically, however, you'd consider the plumbing system as a whole, stop and remember the sound of a toilet flushing right before the temperature shift happened, and conclude that the supply pipes might be small, and that the cold water flow had been temporarily diverted to the toilet; you'd rethink your original assumption that turning up the cold water would make things all right for the rest of your shower, and you'd stand back and wait for the cold water pressure to build again, thus preventing an intense case of goose bumps.

Thinking systemically means that much more of our focus needs to go into how well we work together and how available we are to each other, how we use our critical thinking tools within the context of affirming the communal nature of reality. Our thoughts develop a circulatory system when our focus shifts toward connection and when we begin to think about how one thing affects another, we begin to think about growing more resilient rather than growing bigger; we think about evolving, learning, and developing. Our core image of who we are together reflects the shift in thinking toward relatedness and our

"A human being is part of a 'whole,' called by us 'Universe,' a part limited in time and space. He experiences himself, his thoughts and feelings, as something separate from the rest—a kind of optical delusion of consciousness. This delusion is a kind of prison for us, restricting us to our personal desires and to affection for a few nearest to us. Our task must be to free ourselves from this prison by widening our circle of compassion to embrace all living creatures and the whole of nature in its beauty."
ALBERT EINSTEIN

organization becomes a community, a living ecosystem, since nature originates and organizes more and more complex systems with ease.

Fritjof Capra, in a recent keynote speech, described the ecological principles that are essential for such a sustainable community: interdependency, feedback loops, networking, cyclical patterns, flexibility, diversity, and co-evolution. Dee Hock sums up this reconception: "Any organization is nothing but a mental construction, a concept, an idea to which people and resources are drawn in pursuit of common purpose. All organizations are really, then, conceptual embodiments of a very old and basic idea—the idea of community."

What difference does it make whether we think of ourselves as an organization or a community? If the frontier of the last twenty years was the exploration through inner space and outer space, perhaps we now need to consider the adventure through group space. It is here that we can discover that together. We have the power to change fragmenting ways of thinking into more coherent, integrating, and effective ways of doing and being.

Juanita Brown, president of Whole Systems Associates makes the difference between an organization and a community quite clear: "The fundamental glue of an organization is economic transaction. The glue that holds together a community is the opportunity to make a contribution."

She contrasts them in the following ways: A corporate business is one that is shaped like a pyramid of individual boxes; manned by an army of hired hands, under the command of a CEO with managers who execute an aggressive strategy to attack the competition and expand market share for maximum quarterly financial returns to the stockholders of the corporation.

"The image is a midwife that allows inner wisdom to be birthed into expression."
MATTHEW FOX

A corporate community, on the other hand, is dynamic, linked by networks of interdependent teams; composed of people with diverse characteristics, using all of their talents; guided by shared purpose and quality process, with leaders who are committed to a developmental strategy of environmental scanning linked to continuous learning for improvement, and in the service of maximum long-term customer satisfaction, employee and stockholder enrichment, and the health of the larger society.

"We make a living by what we get, we live by what we give."
WINSTON CHURCHILL

There are no rules or right way to create or evolve this kind of community, any more than there are to love. It takes time, awareness, energy, and the risk and glory of the unpredictable mystery of life. This can be terrifying. This can free us to experiment, to wonder, and to dream. As Harley Davidson describes in their vision of why they are together, "It's the journey, not the destination."

In some ways, this chapter is very much like weaving a web from the strands of all the previous ones. You will have the opportunity to integrate the component skills you have learned into resilient and flexible ways of thinking more inclusively and systemically. The solo practices for mastering oneself are designed to support you in broadening your thinking by expanding your mental models—seeing the whole. The partnered practice for developing mastery with others offers you an experience of perceiving patterns and thinking more generatively, while being constrained by a limiting situation. The group practice for mastering change gives you an experience of thinking inclusively in the complexity and diversity of an organization.

MENTAL MODELS: BE THE CHANGER AND THE CHANGED

A rapidly changing world often requires that we be willing to change our perspective, our mental models the way Vinoba did, as if we were looking through the wide end of a telescope and then flipped it around so we could look the other way, opening our mind like the sky, the whole sense of borders dissolving, our perspective expanding. Our habit, however, is to do exactly the opposite. When confronted by change, we have a tendency to try to maintain our equilibrium by shutting out new information that would disrupt our long-held beliefs and behaviors.

Mental models are cognitive maps, ways we have of thinking about and interpreting experience. Two people will come out of the same meeting, having experienced the same events, and one will shake his/her head saying, "Whew! I'm glad that's over. You just can't win around here." His/her friend, following right behind him/her, can be overheard to say, "That really woke me up. Those new guidelines are going to mean we can take a whole new approach." The only difference between the two is their mental models

Peter Carlson, author and consultant from Healthy Companies, in discussing the current mental model held by many managers that reengineering efforts fail because people resist change—states, "Many of the problems that organizations encounter in this area can be traced back to the assumptions that are being made about people and change, many of which are misleading, outmoded, or simply unfounded."

As an example, he cites a recent study where managers were asked to rank what they think motivates employees the most. They consistently put financial rewards first. Employees, on the other hand, considered financial rewards to be much less important than intrinsic factors, such as meaningful work, fair treatment, and involvement. He concludes that, "Our perceptions of change as positive or negative depend, in large part, on the degree of influence we can exert in a particular situation."

How do we turn the telescope the other way around so we can expand our perspective enough to see where we can have influence, and where we need to inquire into another's model of the world? Many of the principles and practices drawn from the martial arts that you have been experimenting with in this book do just that—make self-mastery a priority to establish a foundation of inner stability you can count on:

- become increasingly more still on the inside as change gathers speed on the outside;

- create space to center, in order to recharge and refresh yourself in the midst of uncertainty, pressure, and upheavals;

- increase your flexibility by maneuvering so that you can choose how you respond to a given situation or person rather than by using manipulation;

- expand your creativity by finding new ways to solve old problems and break obsolete patterns.

RIGHT-BRAINED THINKING IN A LEFT-BRAINED WORLD

You may remember that expanding your periphery is an extremely important support for centering: shifting out of fight or flight by widening your visual field, hearing the sounds around you, and feeling the whole of your body, as well as the energy in the room. From this place, it is possible to develop what we call a multi-point state of awareness that increases your ability

"Those who honestly mean to be true contradict themselves more rarely than those who try to be consistent. "
OLIVER WENDELL HOLMES

to innovate, think generatively, and perceive the whole rather than just the parts. (Although some people insist they are "left-brained," no autopsy has yet revealed a cadaver with only a left brain!)

Find a comfortable position, and notice your breath for a moment. You don't need to change it, just notice each inhale, the space, the exhale, the space, and then the next inhale.

Continue your awareness of your breath, allowing it to include the feeling of your belly. Then increase your awareness so it includes one thing you see and one thing you hear.

You can further expand your awareness, by including two things you see and two things you hear, to your continuing consciousness of your breath and your belly.

You are bringing more and more of the world into you, thinking more and more inclusively. Some of you may want to increase to three things, some of you might find yourself becoming "spacey," as if you are daydreaming or your mind is wandering. That is a signal that your state of mind is expanding and beginning to thinking of a wider range of possibilities and perceive patterns and images rather than analyzing discrete details.

Margaret Wheatley describes her experience in shifting to whole-brained thinking: "First, I try hard to discipline myself to remain aware of the whole and to resist my well-trained desire to analyze the parts to death. I look, now, for the patterns of movement over time and focus on qualities like rhythm, flow, direction, and shape. Second, I know I am wasting time whenever I draw straight arrows between two variables in a cause-and-effect diagram, or position things as polarities, or create elaborate plans and timelines. Third, I no longer argue with anyone about what is real. Fourth, the time I formerly spent on detailed planning and analysis I now use to look at the structures that might facilitate relationships. I have come to expect that something useful occurs if I link up people, units, tasks, even if I cannot determine precise outcomes. And last, I realize more and more that the universe will not cooperate with my desires for determinism."

Metaphoric thinking, including imagery and stories, can reveal these patterns and structures of relationship. The following practice uses the stories you tell yourself, often without realizing you're doing it, to help you find and examine your mental models:

Begin to write or describe an issue or problem you are experiencing. After one paragraph, write the question, "What story am I telling myself about that?" In the next paragraph, dig deep to respond to that question and then go on with your description of the problem. Once again, at the end of the paragraph, write the question, "What story am I telling myself about that?" Continue as long as you find it interesting.

Bert wrote: "I'm having a problem with this new team I'm a part of. They voted me the team leader, but I'm not quite sure what that means or what I'm supposed to do about it."

"What story are you telling yourself about that? "

"I'm telling myself they're going to think I'm a wimp if I don't assert myself soon, and a Nazi if I do. Anyway, so today Marvin wanted to know when our deadline was for the new advertising and all I could think of was to write his question down on the flip chart."

"What story are you telling yourself about that?"

"The hidden wholeness that lies beneath the broken surface of our lives."
THOMAS MERTON

"Well, that I'm really spineless and that they're going to resent me and wonder why I got selected to be leader. This is just like when I was in my last job and. . . ."

When we begin to recognize the patterns of thinking, the stories we tell ourselves, and the mental models that filter our experience, we increase our capacity for freedom and return to our integrity. It is as if we recognize that we are the sky, not the clouds that pass across it. This awareness gives us immediate access to what Victor Frankl called "personal freedom"— our capacity to choose how we respond to any given situation and what meaning it has for us.

The solo practices that follow provide embodied experience of shifting your mental models and increasing your flexibility by expanding your perception of the whole. (Credit to Linda Booth for Part 1 and Moshe Feldenkrais for Part 2.)

"[Truth cannot] be reduced to aphorism or formulas. It is something alive and unpronounceable. Story creates an atmosphere in which it becomes discernible as a pattern."
BARRY LOPEZ

PRACTICE NINETEEN: SOLO
Rotating Mental Models

Part 1
Circles in the Air

Logistics
You will need a pen or pencil

Pick up a pen or pencil. Look up, point the tip toward the ceiling, and draw an imaginary circle in the air. Imagine that the point is tracing a clockwise circle on the ceiling. As you continue to move in that circular motion, slowly lower the

pen down an inch at a time until it is in front of your face.
Continue to lower the revolving pen until you are looking
down on the revolving point.

Notice which way the pen point is now revolving—
clockwise or counterclockwise?

INTEGRATION QUESTIONS

1. What is your initial response to what occurred? Some responses from other people have been, "I think my pen must be broken." "I never did it right in the first place." "This is a trick." "I changed the direction as I brought the pen down. Let me do it again right."

2. What have you been certain about for a period of your life and then later came to embrace a new or even opposite perspective? What was your experience that led to that change in thinking?

Part 2
Improving by Increasing Your Awareness of the Whole

Benchmark: Begin by standing comfortably in a space large enough to allow you to rotate with your arms outstretched. Take care to mark your foot position on the floor in order to keep that constant throughout the practice.

Face forward and choosing one arm, extend it in front of you, and sight along that arm to a point on the wall. Whichever arm you choose, rotate your entire upper body in that same direction as far as you can go, while maintaining your foot position on the floor. For example, if you lift and sight along your left arm, then rotate to the left side. Remember the point on the wall for future reference.

Option 1

Improving by Trying Harder: For the sake of improvement, select one arm and make a greater effort to increase your body's range of motion by vigorously repeating the rotation and stretching in that direction five times.

After that process, test the results of your efforts by benchmarking one more time in that same direction.

Option 2:

Improving by Becoming Aware of Other Aspects of the System: Begin with the same arm and direction as before. Rotate again five times in that direction as before, except for the following: This time, as you rotate your head and neck, arm, and upper body in one direction, let your eyes rotate their gaze in the opposite direction. For example, if your left arm and your body are rotating to the left, your eyes will rotate your gaze to the right.

When you practice changing one variable, you may notice some confusion or awkwardness as your brain rearranges some of its neural pathways. After you have repeated this rotation series five times on the same side as you began, test the results by benchmarking one more time in one direction by sighting along the rotating arm to note where it points to on the walls of the room.

Option 3

Improving by Broadening Your Thinking: Begin with the arm and direction that has not experienced any improvement process. If you began the first two improvement processes with your left arm, practice this third process with your right arm. When you have rotated in that direction as far as possible, make a mental note of where that arm is pointing to on the wall.

Now stand in the beginning position as before and only in your mind, imagine lifting that unimproved arm . . . imagine rotating that unpracticed arm . . . imagine rotating your eyes in the opposite direction, five times.

Notice the results by actually raising that arm and rotating as far a possible until you mentally mark the new maximum point on the wall.

INTEGRATION QUESTIONS

1. Think of one situation at work where you have been applying your most concentrated, diligent efforts and not getting the results you seek.

2. In your attempts to improve, what else could you do besides working harder or longer or concentrating more intensely? What is one factor that you have not even considered as holding improvement potential?

3. Think of one situation at work you avoid because it is uncomfortably strange and awkward or confusing. What's one thing you learned in this practice about being awkward or confused in a learning situation at work?

THINK NETWORKED, ACT BORDERLESS

Parker Palmer describes community as "a capacity for relatedness within individuals—relatedness not only to people, but to events in history, to nature, to the world of ideas and to things of the spirit." What makes this relatedness possible?

"It really boils down to this: that all life is interrelated. We are all caught in an inescapable network of mutuality, tied to a single garment of destiny. Whatever affects one directly affects all indirectly."
MARTIN LUTHER KING

Economist Herman Daly and theologian John Cobb, in their book, *For the Common Good,* explore a reframing of the will to power into forms that build relatedness. "Communal relations are mutual relations in which the norm is not that one loses when another gains, but that each loses in the others' losses and gains in the others. . . . The proper service of community in this case is not sacrificing one's life, but enriching the community through means that enrich oneself as well."

According to Bell's theorem of physics, if you take one particle of a pair from Dallas and move it to London, changing its spin, instantaneously the particle in Dallas will also change its spin. When we move beyond the isolated concept of you and I as separate objects, here and there, we begin to realize, as many other cultures do, that we exist only in relationship to each other. In the Japanese language, for instance, it's not possible to say, "I'm looking at the tree." It is only possible to say, "The tree and I are looking at each other." In the Vietnamese language, you can't speak to someone without making them into a relation of yours. Even if I've never met you before, when I call to you on the road, I'd say, "Older (or younger) brother, how do I get to the next town?"

You can experience this capacity for relatedness through listening in an expanded way:

Find another person and some instrumental music (without words) that is new to both of you and will last for at least five minutes.

Sit back to back in a way that is both comfortable and supportive. As you listen to the music for the first time, notice the images, feelings, and thoughts that pass through you while you listen and for a few minutes in the silence afterwards.

Turn around and share with each other what your experiences were.

Rewind the tape, and repeat the experience, but this time, listen through your partner's ears, trying on their images and experiences. You don't need to lose your own, just add the richness of a whole new way of relating to the music.

Developing a capacity for relatedness also makes it possible to perceive beyond constraints and limitations. In fact, we can develop our ability to use limits beyond our control to foster creative possibilities. Artists know that necessity forces us to improvise with the material at hand, calling up resourcefulness and inventiveness that might not be otherwise possible. A limitation in one direction can provide for total freedom in other directions. The limits of a human hand, how far it will stretch, how quickly it can move, is a structure that imposes a discipline on everything we do with it, from playing a violin to typing on a computer keyboard. The boundaries of a piece of paper are limitations without which any art is not possible. They provide us with something to work with and against. You would not hear an artist putting all of his or her attention on the edges of the paper, moaning and complaining about how it isn't possible to paint beyond them. Rather, they notice the blank paper waiting to be filled.

"The winners of tomorrow will deal proactively with chaos, will look at the chaos per se as the source of market advantage, not as a problem to be got around."
TOM PETERS

In a like manner, there is a basic principle of Aikido that is extremely important for increasing one's perception of the whole. You are asked to notice where you are free as well as where you are stuck or held. This sounds simple, but when we function in relation to others or work, we have been trained to only notice the edges of the paper, to compete with others for who has the biggest sheet, and to struggle to make it bigger.

The practice that follows will give you ample opportunity to shift to thinking of the whole of you—where you are free as well as where you are stuck, and then to the whole of how you are relating to the other.

Noticing Where You Are Free

Benchmark: Think of a work situation in which you are doing your best to make a suggestion, create a new program, or help another person; and, in spite of your best intent and efforts, you are not only feeling ineffective but also attacked. Note the particulars for later reference.

Because you deserve to practice and learn safely and comfortably, Person A signals the pace in this practice.

Person A extends his/her right hand palm up toward person B. Person B reaches out with his/her right hand palm down and *slowly* begins to roll or fold A's fingers back on themselves until the slack is taken out and A calls for a pause.

When A is ready, B begins to *slowly* roll A's fingers even tighter. Person A will notice that even a strong attempt to resist eventually leads to painful resistance and/or collapse.

Both A and B pause, step back, and reflect on what they are most aware of and how they felt about relating to the other in this situation.

When they are ready to begin again, person A practices centering (see chapter 2) and stands in the starting position as before.

Upon a signal from A, B begins to roll up his/her fingers again. At the same time A widens his/her periphery to notice where and how he/she is free to maneuver. Example: His or her fingers and hand may be restrained, but many other parts such as legs, elbows, and feet are free to move.

With that wider awareness, person A can notice what it is like to blend with the downward rolling pressure, by leading the motion with his/her elbow and simultaneously sinking and pivoting.

Having released the downward pressure, person A "feels" for a pathway where movement is possible without clashing with B, where they can both move outward and forward in the same direction without struggle.

Benchmark Revisited: Revisit that situation at work where your best efforts are leading to ineffective and painful results. What is the energy or movement that you are fighting against? Notice where you are free to move in the same direction of the energy in order to release some pressure, to learn more about the other person's needs, and to then influence them in a whole new direction where both your energies are aligned.

Opposing energy is wasteful. A system is more efficient when all energy is joined in the same direction. In this situation, how have you, even in your best efforts, been adding to the struggle? What is one thing you could do to move from being "right" to being "effective?"

INTEGRATION QUESTIONS

1. As person A, what helped you notice the system as a whole; that is, your discomfort, B's energy and direction, the places where your body was not trapped, directions in which you could move, how you could comfortably remain connected to B, instead of going into fight of flight?

2. As person B, what was the effect when the contracted energy you were applying to A's hand suddenly released and went in a new direction?

"The drop of water is only weak when it is removed from the ocean."
BAIRD T. SPAULDING

A COLLECTION OF INTELLIGENCES OR A COLLECTIVE INTELLIGENCE?

We have been exploring ways of expanding our perception of the patterns which form the invisible architecture of the whole. As you continue widening, the conventional notion of who you are, the limited and isolated notion of the self begins to become unhinged. You shift to what can be called "contextual perception"—surveying the context within which our lives take place. You don't just see the whole, you become it.

Try this little reflective experiment of witnessing your own context and noticing how you are affected by it:

Consider thinking of your genetic inheritance, both personal and as a member of a species. Reflect on the fact that your existence is the culmination of millions of years of preparation. Deep in your flesh and bones resides a constant and reliable source of encouragement from the ancestors whose passions brought you into being and who want life to evolve. Your very existence is the culmination of millions of years of preparation. If all those life forms that stand behind you could speak, they would express a hope that their lives have contributed to something wonderful. All of life supports your best effort and is rooting for your success. This is the inherent affirmation of every positive step you take. That which is ancient, is also newly born in you.

"The whole world lives within a safe guarding. Fish inside the waves, birds held in the sky, the elephant, the ant, the waiting snake, the ground, the water, the spark—all exist and are held in this great divine. Nothing is ever alone for a single moment."
RUMI

But how do you perceive the whole of such a complex context as a modern corporate community? In just one organization of eighty thousand employees, the director of human resources concluded that there were more than one hundred diverse cultures and ethnic group represented in their workforce.

Organizational consultant and author, Judy Sorum Brown, describes the challenges of thinking inclusively in the midst of such diversity: "We must consider that when one of us is left out, is not present around the table, a portion of each of ourselves is lost as well. When the slave is victimized, so is the master. When the women's voice is deleted, so is the tiny voice within men who also yearn to speak out for time to care, for a greater sense of connectedness, and for ties with their children and broader family. When the man in the wheelchair is invisible, we all risk invisibility. When the African vision, or the Native American vision of the world goes unrepresented, also lost to each of us is that part of our own vision that sprang from the same place on earth. The loss represented in a lack of diversity is not just a loss to the collective well-being. It is a very deep and personal loss of ourselves, and within ourselves as well."

So how do we allow different mental models to coexist and be examined noncompetitively? How do we become realistic visionaries who can recognize the talents, intelligence, and creativity that diverse organizational members bring to their work. How do we build on this diversity to inspire greater commitment and achievement? How do we coordinate sustained efforts for improvement in systemic issues where mandates from the top will never work?

Both of the words "community" and "communicate" are rooted in the same meaning: to be connected. As we search for ways to increase our effectiveness working together in teams and leading collaboratively, we inevitably find ourselves limited by the rigid and habitual ways we have to communicate with each other. Is there a form that can help us "flock"? Is there a way to help us do what Leonard Bernstein described music doing: "Name the unnamable and communicate the unknowable?"

Ikujiro Nonaka in an article in *Harvard Business Review* entitled "The Knowledge Creating Company," described the importance of communication for teams in the emerging organizational learning community: "Teams provide a shared context where individuals can interact with each other and engage in the constant dialogue on which effective reflection depends. Team members pool their information and examine it from various angles. Eventually, they integrate their diverse individual perspectives into a new collective perspective."

"The seat of a soul is not inside a person or outside a person but the very place they overlap and meet with the world."
GERARD DE NERVAL

"Behind every helplessness, there's a yearning."
PETER SENGE

Organizations such as General Electric, EDS, and Polaroid, to name a few, are led by teams of executives rather than one "great individual." Charles Keifer of Innovations Associates, says of them, "Collective leadership is as different from individual leadership as collective learning is from individual learning. Mastering team leadership means mastering a more complex agenda. There needs to be alignment around shared vision, the ability to discuss current reality, a clarity of roles, and methods for capturing and assessing collective knowledge. The ability to dialogue openly and truthfully is essential."

Chris Thorsen, a leadership consultant on the west coast who coaches executive leaders with methods drawn from Aikido and dialogue, describes why this ability to communicate in a different way is so significant for leadership teams: "It inevitably becomes necessary for members to reveal more of the truth than is normally comfortable. Their underlying fear, from the Aikido perspective, is actually the harbinger of power. If they can free up the energy by centering, opening and flowing with change, then team members can safely share the vital information that too often goes uncommunicated for fear of misunderstanding or reprisal. They learn a safe way to reveal the truth and set their power free."

The critical error that most teams seem to make is the assumption that a command and control culture can change to an empowered one by using command and control methods. What it needs instead is a consensual methodology to facilitate a self-organizing evolution. This involves bringing together relevant stakeholders across the system to create a collaborative context for the shared culture in which communication can happen.

Whenever people perceive that their voice is heard, their opinions respected, their contributions valued, then their participation increases. What most people call listening, however, according to Judy Brown, is usually just listening to test for rightness or fit with their own beliefs, and then to defend or maintain their position. In addition to the familiar sequence of data gathering and analytic problem solving, what is needed is a more iterative process of exploration, deliberation, and integrative dialogue among people in multiple configurations.

irimi = *moving into a situation, embracing life, developing deeper contact, entering fully into life situations*

For this to happen, we need to learn to engage with each other at much deeper levels. Both dialogue and Aikido are arts of open inquiry that support this. Dialogue is a collective wondering, which uncovers key questions, encourages diverse points of view, reveals and challenges assumptions, explores where the known meets the unknown, and senses for the emergent current of meaning. Physicist David Bohm was a significant modern proponent of this ancient form. Dialogue is not the same as discussion, which searches for closure and decision. Drawing on insight rather than knowledge, it recognizes and clears up the incoherence of thought within and between us. Thus, it offers the possibility that we may learn to truly speak from the "I" and listen from the "we," respectful witnesses to the individual and collective process of learning.

The practice that follows is an opportunity to practice what in Aikido is called *rei,* which means both respect and gratitude—respect for an awareness of the process a group needs to learn collectively and respect for an effectiveness a community needs to develop to function and accomplish productively. And gratitude? Gratitude for the richness that diversity brings to us, the 360 degrees that can make collaboration a work of art.

PRACTICE TWENTY-ONE: GROUP

Warped Juggle

(credit to Linda Booth)

Logistics

A group of 8–12 people in a space cleared of furniture or other obstructions, large enough for people to stand shoulder-to-shoulder. The only materials you will need are three soft tossable objects like beanbags or "koosh" balls.

⑥ Gather the group into a circle with one person acting as the intiatior. The initiator introduces one of the tossable objects and begins by gently tossing it to another member across the circle.

⑥ The person who catches the first toss then throws it to someone else across the circle, who has yet to touch it, and so on, until every member of the group has caught and tossed the ball and it is returned to the facilitator.

⑥ Repeat the sequence with each member remembering to whom they tossed the object.

⑥ After the initial sequence has been practiced with one object, the initiator adds the second and then the third object to the tossing so three objects are simultaneously being tossed in sequence.

⑥ Ask the group to improve upon the time it takes to exchange all three objects in sequence. As people experiment to improve upon the time to complete the task, there are two constants which must be respected: 1) Everyone in the circle must touch each object once, and 2) they must be touched in the same sequence. Note: If any member has done this practice before, they can silently participate as the others create new improvement strategies.

⑥ The group estimates the amount of time they think their best effort will take and chooses a timer with a stopwatch to record their attempts. The tossing sequence is begun again by an initiator saying *go*. When the initiator receives all three objects, he/she signals *stop*.

Typically the first round of practice takes 20–40 seconds. During the practice, one person can elect to stand outside the circle and make process comments like, "What happened when someone offered a new idea? What patterns of behavior did you observe? What problem-solving assumptions surfaced?" The group can also address these questions collectively after completing the practice.

INTEGRATION QUESTIONS

1. How did you use the improvement strategy of increasing effort? How much improvement did that strategy bring? What were some signs of the breakdown of that strategy, the constraint or limit in that initial pattern of success? For example, the group may have decided to squeeze in tighter or to throw the ball faster which may have initially produced some improvement, but eventually led to more errors, dropped objects, and delays. What corollary can you make to a work situation?

2. What kinds of inherent blind spots, pressures, and constraints occurred in the group as a result of its initial success? How is a successful pattern on your job stagnating your thinking or making you unaware of possibilities?

3. How did the initial presentation of the task color the team's creative-thinking process? Think about a situation at work where the initial assessment or presentation of a problem led the company or department on a "wild goose chase" before a solution was finally reached.

BUSINESS ANECDOTE

A group of administrators from a large health care system used practice twenty-one, The Warped Juggle, to develop an awareness of how to work within all of the complexities of their system. There were eight groups of about fifteen people. Even though the two constraints were spoken and written, one group continued for most of the allotted time tossing the ball as had been demonstrated at the beginning. They showed greatly improved time and had a lot of fun, but never redesigned their structure to meet the constraints in a more efficient way as did other groups. They admitted that this was true of their unit at work—in service they experienced great team spirit and enjoyment, but not a lot of innovation or rethinking of processes.

Another group immediately understood that their structure could be redesigned. They tried the way they were directed at first, and then spent up until the very last minute planning and accomplished the task in five seconds. But even with this great time, there was some discomfort with their process. They noticed how a few vocal members did most of the planning. Lots of ideas were disregarded, and there wasn't much experiential learning. Several members said they felt left out of the creative loop, and probably would withdraw their energy if they had to continue. They realized that, in their unit, there were a few super planners and many quiet "compliers." Over time this configuration produced withholding of resources and dependency on a few.

What surfaced was an awareness that short-term success was only a small part of the overall learning curve. Variables were defined that had never been considered before the challenge, such as participants' desire to continue learning and improving in the future, the use of inquiry in the design strategies, and the ability to hold to two or three states of consciousness at the same time.

"Never doubt that a small group of thoughtful, committed citizens can change the world. Indeed it is the only thing that ever has."
MARGARET MEAD

9

What is the coherence that exists beyond fragmentation?

A CLOSING

Creating a New Ecology of Caring

"*If you are a poet, you will see clearly that there is a cloud floating in this sheet of paper. Without a cloud there will be no water; without water, the trees cannot grow; and without trees, you cannot make paper. So the cloud is in here. . . . Let us think of other things, like sunshine. Sunshine is very important because the forest cannot grow without sunshine, and we as humans cannot grow without sunshine. So the logger needs sunshine in order to cut the tree, and the tree needs sunshine in order to be a tree. Therefore you can see sunshine in this sheet of paper. And if you look more deeply . . . you see not only the cloud and the sunshine in it, but that everything is here, the wheat that became the bread for the logger to eat, the logger's father—everything is in this sheet of paper. . . . The presence of this tiny sheet of paper proves the presence of the whole cosmos.*"

THICH NHAT HANH, *Being Peace*

The survival of our species is predicated on one major distinguishing characteristic—flexibility. We can find our lost organizational integrity by expanding our ability to let go of our preconceptions and extending our ability to receive the other's perspective. That's what flexibility is.

If knowing the righteous answers can fragment us, asking the sacred questions is what can connect us. In the legend of the Holy Grail, Parsifal (sometimes called Gawaine) is on his way to become a knight in King Arthur's castle, when he finds himself in the middle of a wasteland, where everything is degenerating, sterile. At the castle he discovers that the king has been wounded in the groin and thus has also lost the powers of regeneration. The courtiers and inhabitants are in a spell, moving on automatic, doing nothing about the wasteland.

Parsifal has no answers, but his head is filled with questions. He's been told he can awaken them all by asking the right questions. But he remembers his mother's constant injunction not to embarrass people by asking questions so he leaves the castle and wasteland. After much pain and struggle, he returns. This time, he overcomes his hesitancy and asks, "What aileth thee?" and "Whom doth thou serve?" The spell is broken and all becomes revitalized.

What would happen in your corporate community if you asked a modern-day version of Parsifal's questions and listened from your heart? What if you asked various members, "What do you consider to be the biggest danger we're facing? Do you think there's something a person like you can do about it? What gives you hope?"

To be heard in this way is a gift. To tell our stories a necessity. To listen to the stories of others, a source of the community's

"Our deepest fear is not that we are inadequate. Our deepest fear is that we are powerful beyond measure. It is our light, not our darkness, that most frightens us. We ask ourselves, who am I to be brilliant, gorgeous talented and fabulous? Actually, who are you not to be?"
NELSON MANDELA

collective wisdom. Gandhi used to describe a "truth force" that has tremendous power to unite people. To understand a system, you have to understand its vulnerabilities. Truth does not exist inside of us or even just outside of us. It exists also between us. When we tell the truth to each other about what we feel and see and know is happening, an immense vitality is released—we awaken. What if we considered this awakening to be development—waking to our true wealth and potential as persons and as a society? What if we awakened to our real needs for connection, our capacity to work together, and to our power to evolve? What if we awakened to discover that we don't have to invent our connections? They already exist in the "hidden wholeness." What if we awakened to discover that we belong to each other?

"In life, the issue is not control, but dynamic interconnected-ness. I want to act from that knowledge. . . . I want to surrender my care of the universe and become a participating member, with everyone I work with, in an organization that moves gracefully with its environment, trusting in the unfolding dance of order."
ERIC JANTSCH

E MALAMA I KO OLA KINO—RESPECT YOUR BODY

Hawaiian Proverb

APPENDIX

The Five Disciplines of a Learning Organization

MENTAL MODELS

Imagine you are wearing sunglasses. You put them on for a long day at the beach. When you come home you are so tired that you forget to take them off. You fall asleep with them perched on your nose. When you awaken the next morning, you are not aware that you have them on. They feel quite natural, and the tinted world begins to seem normal. Hours, days, weeks go by. No one mentions to you that you are wearing sunglasses, assuming you must have a good reason for shielding your eyes. One day, twenty years later, something happens to increase your awareness. Perhaps a child asks why you wear sunglasses all the time, or you get sick and, at the hospital you have to check all your worldly possessions at the main desk. Your glasses are snatched from your face and you are blinded without your accustomed filters.

You close your eyes and keep them that way until it is time to leave and the glasses are returned to you. Although you are not willing to give them up, your curiosity grows about what the world would be like without them. You go to a store and buy the elastic strings that slip over the ear pieces so you can take the sunglasses off from time to time, for a moment or two, and notice what unfiltered awareness is like. Now, you have a choice that you previously were not aware you had.

This describes the discipline of "mental models," except substitute the words *belief systems* for sunglasses. Here we examine the deeply embedded assumptions we make about how the world is, and notice how they shape our actions and decisions. The elastic strings represent the new kinds of conversations we learn to carry on that balance inquiry and advocacy. In this way we can reflect on and improve the perspective we have of the world.

Our minds run on ideas the way cars run on gasoline. When we get outside of our mental constructions, observing our own thinking, we enrich our fuel supply. Instead of limiting possibilities into one right answer, we expand our thinking by generating a multiplicity of possibilities?

PERSONAL MASTERY

This is the discipline of continually clarifying and deepening our personal aspiration, our ability to create the results we most desire, while simultaneously increasing our awareness of the current reality of our situation in order to learn how our actions affect the world around us.

There is a great deal of emphasis in business on envisioning a positive future. There is little attention, however, given to perceiving the current reality clearly and telling the truth about it.

Moshe Feldenkrais stated, "When you really know what and how you are doing, you can learn whatever you want." When you discover how you are triggering your reactive, fight or flight response to a particular situation--for instance, by how you are talking, focusing your eyes, or tensing your muscles—it becomes relatively easy to do the opposite.

TEAM LEARNING

Historically, we've viewed learning as an individual endeavor, but the complexity of the present demands that we accelerate our ability to create a synergy as we learn together on the job. In the early part of this decade, we implemented Quality Improvement Teams, but evaluating their effectiveness yields greater promises than results.

In sports and the performing arts, two fields where teams learn reliably and collaboratively, players move regularly between a practice field (rehearsal) and the "real" game (performance). But this capacity to learn together does not transfer to the arena of business.

The discipline of team learning enables the development of collective intelligence beyond the reach of any individual. Its practice involves aligning and developing the capacity of a team to create the results its members truly desire. It includes conversational and collaborative thinking skills so that groups of people can reliably develop ability greater than the sum of individual members' talents.

In a recent study by Rosabeth Moss Kanter and associates published in the *Harvard Business Review* of thirty-seven global companies, it was found that a well-developed ability to create and sustain fruitful collaborations gives companies a competitive leg up in the new economy. But our unconscious incompetence at relational thinking is showing in the workplace, as it does the home. The researchers observed that "North American companies, more than any others in the world, take a narrow, opportunistic view of relationships, evaluating them strictly in financial terms, neglecting frequently the political, cultural, organizational, and human aspects of partnership. They are the most adept at exploiting them." Being a good partner has become a key corporate asset to be nurtured.

SHARED VISION

The discipline of shared vision builds a sense of commitment in a group by developing the core images of the future its members seek to create, and the principles and guiding practices by which they hope to get there. It is not possible to move into a collaborative approach to life with images and metaphors which are war-like, involving winning and losing, machines and battlefields.

Our minds make meaning through symbol, metaphor, and analogy. They help us think about the whole of things, help people find connections by relating something strange and unknown to their own experience. They help uncover patterns in apparent chaos. One California consulting firm whose special area of interest was collaborative-team-building found its own employees in a state of polarization. Two hours of listening with awareness by someone not involved in the company revealed that the leadership continually used football metaphors at every meeting, implicitly pitting one team against the other. When we suggested holding a meeting where all the metaphors related to sailing, such as, "We are all in this boat together," "Who's going to chart the course?" "How do we sail in a wind this stiff without capsizing?" the climate changed from one of implicit competition to explicit cooperation. We must change our inner lens so we can begin to see anew with images that can transform our consciousness.

The amount of information that is known by human beings doubles every five years. Information is like a river. Even if you step in at exactly the same place you did a day ago, what will be flowing past you will be completely different. We need to learn to approach problems with a continually changing current of information. But that is not all. We are being challenged. As Carolyn Lukensmeyer, Director of America Speaks, reminds us to ask ourselves, "What is the legacy that our generation will leave? Will we be known as the Information Age? Or will we be known as the Age of Consciousness?" This is the domain of shared vision.

SYSTEMS THINKING

This is the discipline that integrates all the others. It is a way of thinking that seeks to find the structures underlying complex situations, enabling us to see the interrelationships, the patterns of change and action required for sustainable improvement. It gives us a language with which to understand and describe the forces that shape the behavior of systems. Thus we discover how to act more in harmony with the larger processes of the natural and economic world in which we are embedded.

Systems thinking has its roots in the 1920s in the work of gestalt psychology, cybernetics, and the beginnings of ecological thinking. It was more fully developed in the seventies and eighties as knowledge grew about life being organized in what Margaret Wheatley, author of *Leadership and the New Science* calls "self-organizing systems." She says, "We began to shift our basic way of seeing reality—a change in our scientific world view from one of discrete, measurable objects to one of interwoven relationships."

This shift presents many dilemmas. Dick Cross, former CEO of Halcyon Corp. and now consultant and advisor to other CEOs, describes one: "I spent 50 percent of my time helping individuals or groups get their heads on straight—helping them understand collective goals, what's motivating someone else, their own role, how others perceive them, where they can help, and where they need help. This time was spent absorbing and understanding their energy and redirecting it. Today, most of the job of a CEO or GM is being someone to talk to about how to deal with people. The rest of the job is thinking about strategy and finance. This is the reverse of how American management has been thinking since the 1950s. The relational issues are the big unknown. Pretty much everyone knows how to deal with the technical stuff—but we've forgotten or never knew how to deal with people.

"Reading and feeling other people's energy and redirecting or channeling it in a different direction is most of the job. It's a new idea for a CEO to collaborate, confide, and reach out to others to simulate scenarios, to notice what feels best, to ask for input to help think about it. Mostly anyone educated in management in the last thirty years has been learning the wrong stuff."

BIBLIOGRAPHY

Ackoff, Russell L. *The Art Of Problem Solving*. New York: John Wiley & Sons, Inc., 1978.

Alon, Ruth. *Mindful Spontaneity*. New York: Avery Publishing Group, 1991.

Argyris, Chris. *Knowledge For Action.* San Francisco: Jossey-Bass Publishers, 1993.

Argyris, Chris. *Overcoming Organizational Defenses*. New York: Allyn & Bacon, 1990.

Benson, Roger. "Cutting Edge: Mapping the Learning Landscape." *Organizations and People,* Issue 1, Volume 4.

Berman, Morris. *Coming To Our Senses.* New York: Bantam Books, 1990.

Bridges, William. *Managing Transitions.* New York: Addison-Wesley Publishing, Co., 1991.

Brown, Judy S., *The Choice: Seasons Of Loss and Renewal After A Father's Decision To Die.* Berkley, California: 1995.

Chawla, Sarita and Kenesch, John. *Learning Organizations.* Portland, O r - egon: Productivity Press, Inc., 1995.

Collins, James C. *Built To Last.* New York: Harper Business, 1994.

Covey, Stephen R., Merrill, A, Roger and Merrill, Rebecca R. *First Things First.* New York: Simon & Shuster, 1994.

Crum, Thomas F., *The Magic of Conflict.* New York: Touchstone, Simon & Shuster, 1987.

Davidow, William H. and Malone, Michael S. *The Virtual Corporation.* New York: Edward Burlingame Books, Harper Business, 1992.

Dobson, Terry and Miller, Victor. *Aikido in Everyday Life.* Berkeley, California: North Atlantic Books, 1993.

Dobson, Terry and Moss, Rikki. *Between Love, Trust and Surrender.* Grand Isle, Vermont: Rikki Moss, 1994.

_____. *It's Alot Like Dancing.* California: Frog, Ltd., 1993.

Dobson, Terry. *When Push Comes to Shove.* Self-Published, 1980.

Drucker, Peter F. *Post-Capitalist Society.* New York: HarperBusiness, 1993.

Eisler, Riane. *The Chalice and The Blade.* CSan Francisco: Harper San Francisco, 1987.

Feldenkrais, Moshe. *Awareness Through Movement.* New York: Harper and Row, 1977.

Fox, Matthew. *The RE-Invention of Work.* New York: Harper Collins, 1994.

Fritz, Robert. *The Path of Least Resistance, Revised.* New York: Ballantine Books, 1989.

Goldstein, Jeffery. *The Unshackled Organization.* Portland, Oregon: Productivity Press, Inc., 1994.

Hanna, Thomas. *Somatics.* New York: Addison-Wesley Publishing Co., 1988.

Hawkin, Paul. *Growing A Business.* New York: Fireside Books, Simon & Shuster, Inc., 1987.

Heckler, Richard Strozzi. *The Anatomy Of Change.* Boston, Massachussetts: Shambala Publications, Inc., 1984.

Homma, Gaka. *Aikido For Life.* Berkeley, California: North Atlantic Books, 1987.

Joiner, Brian L. *Fourth Generation Management.* New York: McGraw-Hill, Inc., 1994.

Kantor, Rosabeth, M. "Collaborative Advantage." *Harvard Business Review,* July-August 1994.

Kelly, Kevin. *Out Of Control.* New York: Addison-Wesley Publishing Co., 1994.

Klickstein, Bruce. *Living Aikido.* California: North Atlantic Books, 1987.

Kofman, Fred and Senge, Peter. "Communities of Commitment: The Heart of the Learning Organization." *American Management Association,* 1993.

Lambert, Craig. "Leadership In A New Way." *Harvard Magazine,* March/

April 1995.

Lelen, Kenneth. "Managing With Soul." *Publisher's Weekly*, August 1, 1994.

Leornard, George. *Mastery.* New York: Penguin Books, 1991.

Markova, Dawna, Ph.D. *The Art of the Possible, A Compassionate Approach to Understanding the Way People Think, Learn and Communicate.* Berkeley, California: Conari Press, 1990.

_____. *How Your Child Is Smart: A Life Changing Approach to Learning.* Berkeley, California: Conari Press, 1992.

_____. *No Enemies Within: A Creative Process for Discovering What's Right About What's Wrong.* Berkeley, California: Conari Press, 1994.

McGartland, Grace. *Thunderbolt Thinking.* Texas, Bernard-Davis Publishing Co., 1994.

Mindell, Arnold, Ph.D. *The Leader As Martial Artist.* San Francisco: HarperSanFrancisco, 1992.

Murphy, Michael. *The Future of the Body.* New York: G.P. Putnam and Sons, 1992

O'Rielly, Brian. "The New Deal: What Companies and Employees Owe One Another." *Fortune Magazine,* June 13,1994.

Pater, Robert. "Black Belt Moves to Management." *Personnel Administrator,* Nov. 1989.

Reed, William. *Ki: A Road That Anyone Can Walk.* New York: Japan Publications Inc., 1986.

_____. *Ki: A Practice Guide for Westerners.* New York: Japan Publications Inc., 1986.

Richards, Dick. *Artful Work.* San Francisco: Berrett-Koehler Publishers, Inc. 1995

Schwartz, Peter. *The Art of the Long View.* New York: Currency/Doubleday, 1991.

Senge, Peter. *The Fifth Discipline Fieldbook.* New York: Currency/ Doubleday, 1994.

Sherman, Stratford. "Leaders Learn to Heed the Voice Within." *Fortune Magazine,* August 22, 1994.

Srivastra, Suresh and Copperrider, David and Associates. *Appreciative Management and Leadership.* San Francisco: Jossey-Bass Publishers, 1990.

Stevens, John. *Aikido: The Way Of Harmony.* Boston, Massachussetts: Shambala Publications, 1984.

_____. *Abundant Peace.* Boston, Massachussetts: Shambala Publications, 1987.

_____. *The Secret Of Aikido.* Boston, Massachussetts: Shambala Publications, 1995.

Stewart, Thomas A. "Intellectual Capital." *Fortune Magazine,* October, 3, 1994.

Tohei, Koichi. *Ki In Daily Life.* Tokyo, Japan: KI NO Kenkyuka H.Q., 1978.

Vaill, Peter. *Managing as a Performing Art.* San Francisco: Jossey-Bass Inc., Publishers, 1989.

Ventura, Michael, "The Age of Interruption." *Networker,* January/February 1995.

Watzlawick, Paul, Ph.D. and Weakland, John, Ch.E. and Fisch, Richard, M.D. *Change.* New York: W.W. Norton & Company, Inc., 1974.

Weisbord, Marvin R. and 35 International Co-Authors. *Discovering Common Ground.* San Francisco: Berrett-Koehler Publishers, 1992.

Westbrook, Adele and Ratte, Oscar. *AIKIDO and the Dynamic Sphere.* Rutland, Vermont. Charles E. Tuttle, Co., 1987.

Wheatley, Margaret. *Leadership and the New Science.* San Francisco: Berrett-Koehler Publishers, Inc., 1995.

Wheatley, Margaret and Senge, Peter. "The Learning Organization: From Vision to Reality." *The Systems Thinker,* Vol.4, No. 10 1993.

Wilson, John. "Managing Change." *Retreat,* Issue No. 5.

Other Resources

Alon, Ruth. "The Grammar Of Spontaneity." Felldenkrais Resources, Berkeley: 1990.

Bailyn, Lotte. "The Impact of Corporate Culture on Work-Family Integration" *Lecture: Sloan School of Management, M.I.T.,* November 16, 1994.

Booth, Linda. *The System Thinking Playbook.* Contact the author for more information: 11 Sophia Drive, Uxbridge, MA 01569.

Brown, Juanita and Bennett, Sherrin. "Strategic Dialogue, Strengthening Collaborative Learning, Insight and Innovation." *Pre-publication draft: The Learning Organization.* New Leader's Press, April 18, 1994.

Brown, Judy S. "Empowerment: Being Of Two Minds About Leadership" *Working Paper Series,* 1992.

Thorsen, Chris and Richard Moon. "Harmonious Leadership" *An Interview: The Performance Edge.*

Aikido Dojo

(Contact these dojo for information about smaller outlying dojo.)

Austin Ki Society, Kathey Ferland, 211 W. North Loop, Austin, TX 78757, 512-459-9249

Bay Area Ki Society, Pietro Yuji Maida, 2525 Eighth Street #12, Berkeley, CA:: 94710, 510-848-3437

Chicago Ki Society, John Eley, 1019 Diversey Parkway, Chicago, IL, 60614, 312-721-9006

Midland Ki Society, Vic Montgomery, P.O.B. 1033, Shawne Mission, KS 66222, 913-362-7314

Maui Aikido Ki Society, Shinichi Suzuki, P.O. Box 724, Wailuku, Maui, HI 96796, 808-575-2367

New Jersey Ki Society, Terrence Pierce, 529 Howard Streed, Riverton, NJ 08077, 609-829-7323

Northwest Ki Federation, Calvin Tabata, P.O. Box 2143, Lake Oswego, OR 97035, 503-684-0185

Rocky Mountain Ki Society, Russell Jones, 2400 30th Street, Boulder, CO 80302, 303-442-0505

Seattle Ki Society, Koichi Kashiwaya, 6106 Roosevelt Way N.E., Seattle, WA 98115, 206-527-2151

Southern California Ki Society, Clarence Chinn, P.O. Box 3752, Gardena, CA 90247, 310-514-8834

South Carolina Ki Society, Dr. David Shaner, Dept. of Philosophy, Furman University, Greenville, SC 29613, 803-269-4664

Vermont Aikido, Ken Nisson, 274 North Winooski Avenue, Burlington, VT 05401, 802-862-9785.

Aikido of Montpelier, Sara Norton, 7 Court Street, Third Floor, Montpelier, VT 05602, 802-454-8550.

Virginia Ki Society, George Simcox, 5631 Cornish Way, Alexandria, VA 22310, 703-971-7928

INDEX

If you found *An Unused Intelligence* useful, chances are you will enjoy Dr. Dawna Markova's other books:

No Enemies Within: *A Creative Process for Discovering What's Right about What's Wrong*

How Your Child is Smart: *A Life-Changing Approach to Learning*

The Art of the Possible: *A Compassionate Approach to Understanding the Way People Think, Learn & Communicate*

Andy Bryner and Dr. Markova are available for consultations.

To order books, or to contact Mr. Bryner and Dr. Markova, please write, call, fax, or e-mail Conari Press at:

CONARI PRESS

2550 Ninth Street, Suite 101
Berkeley, CA 94710
Phone: 800–685–9595
Fax: 510–649–7190
e–mail: conaripub@aol.com